TITLE I/PSEN ENGLISH

# APPARITIONS

**21 Stories of Ghosts, Spirits, and Mysterious Manifestations—
With Exercises for Developing Critical Reading Skills**

John F. Warner
Margaret B. Warner

Jamestown Publishers
Providence, Rhode Island

**APPARITIONS**
**21 Stories of Ghosts, Spirits, and Mysterious Manifestations—**
**With Exercises for Developing Critical Reading Skills**

Catalog No. 766
Copyright ©1987 by Jamestown Publishers

Cover Illustration by Bob Eggleton
Cover and Text Design by Deborah Hulsey Christie

Printed in the United States AL

88 89 90 91 9 8 7 6 5 4 3 2

ISBN 0-89061-465-2

# Contents

To the Teacher  **5**

  Introduction

  How to Use This Book

Sample Unit  **10**

To the Student  **16**

## GROUP ONE

  1  The Bell Witch  **18**

  2  The Gray Man of Pawley's Island  **24**

  3  The Flying Dutchman  **30**

  4  The Ghosts of Flight 401  **36**

  5  Ocean-born Mary  **42**

  6  The Case of the Missing Secretary  **48**

  7  The Ghost Ship of Matthew Lee  **54**

## GROUP TWO

  8  Osceola's Head  **62**

  9  Whaley House  **68**

10  The Marine Lieutenant's Ghost  **74**

11  The Haunted Gold Mine  **80**

12  Sarah's Ghost House  **86**

13  The Ghost Ship of Georges Bank  **92**

14  Harvey of Fort Sam Houston  **98**

## GROUP THREE

15   The Return of Nelly Butler   **106**

16   A Beverly Hills Ghost   **112**

17   The Haunted U-Boat   **118**

18   Lady in Black   **124**

19   The Yankee Poltergeist   **130**

20   Testimony of a Ghost in Court   **136**

21   Spiritualism: Fact or Fraud?   **142**


Answer Key   **150**

Words per Minute Table   **154**

Progress Graphs

    Reading Speed   **156**

    Critical Reading Scores   **157**


Picture Credits   **158**

# To the Teacher

## INTRODUCTION

Judging by the enormous popularity of books and movies dealing with the occult, many people are intrigued by the subject of spirits—of an existence after death. *Apparitions* capitalizes on that interest to get your students reading—and to keep them reading.

*Apparitions* features tales of ghosts and poltergeists—some helpful, some harmless, some sinister, some with a grudge, some with a mission. The tales range from the legendary to the contemporary. A few of the sightings and events have been substantially documented with testimonies by witnesses, others offer little in the way of proof or support. Some have been shown to be frauds, some live on as a mixture of fact and legend, some have stood up to intensive investigation and remain a mystery. The stories are not a collection of "ghost stories" in the traditional sense—they do not try to frighten the reader or to present the apparitions as authentic. Rather, they are *accounts of* ghost stories. The approach is journalistic.

*Apparitions* provides subject matter for thoughtful interpretation and discussion, while challenging your students in four critical reading categories: main idea, important details, inferences, and vocabulary in context. *Apparitions* can also help your students to improve their reading rates. Timing of the selections is optional, but many teachers find it an effective motivating device.

*Apparitions* consists of twenty-one units divided into three groups of seven units each. All the stories in a group are on the same reading level. Group One is at the sixth-grade reading level, Group Two at the seventh, and Group Three at the eighth, as assessed by the Fry Formula for Estimating Readability.

## HOW TO USE THIS BOOK

**Introducing the Book.** This text, used creatively, can be an effective tool for learning certain critical reading skills. We suggest that you begin by introducing the students to the contents and format of the book. Examine the book with the students to see how it is set up and what it is about. Discuss the title. What is an apparition? (In this book, apparitions include not only visions of ghostly beings and things, but also evidence of spirits, such as voices and noises that emanate from no known source, and objects that appear or move about on their own.) Read through the table of contents as a class, to gain an overview of the apparitions that will be encountered.

**The Sample Unit.** To learn what is contained in each unit and how to proceed through a unit, turn to the Sample Unit on pages 10–15. After you have examined these pages yourself, work through the Sample Unit with your students, so that they may have a clear understanding of the purpose of the book and of how they are to use it.

The Sample Unit is set up exactly as the regular units are. At the beginning there is a photograph or illustration accompanied by a brief introduction to the story. The story is next, followed by four types of comprehension exercises: Finding the Main Idea, Recalling Facts, Making Inferences, and Using Words Precisely.

Begin by having someone in the class read aloud the introduction that appears with the picture. Then give the students a few moments to study the picture. Ask for their thoughts on what the story will be about. Continue the discussion for a minute or so. Then have the students read the story. (You may wish to time the students' reading, in order to help them improve their reading speed as well as their comprehension. A Words per Minute table is located in the back of the book, to help the students figure their reading rates.)

Then go through the sample questions as a class. An explanation of the comprehension skill and directions for answering the questions are given at the beginning of each exercise. Make sure all the students understand how to answer the four different types of questions and how to figure their scores. The correct answers and sample scores are filled in. Also, explanations of all the correct answers are given within the sample Main Idea and Making Inferences exercises, to help the students understand how to think through these question types.

As the students are working their way through the Sample Unit, be sure to have them turn to the Words per Minute table on pages 154 and 155 (if you have timed their reading) and the Reading Speed and Critical Reading Scores graphs on pages 156 and 157 at the appropriate points. Explain to the students the purpose of each, and read the directions with them. Be sure they understand how the table and graphs will be used. You will probably have to help them find and mark their scores for the first unit or two.

**Timing the Story.** If you are going to time your students' reading, explain to them your reason for doing so: to help them keep track of and improve their reading rates.

Here's one way of timing. Have all the students in the class begin reading the story at the same time. After one minute has passed, write on the chalkboard the time that has elapsed, and begin updating it at ten-second intervals (1:00, 1:10, 1:20, etc.). Tell the students to copy down the last time shown on the chalkboard when they have finished reading. They should write their reading time in the space designated after the story.

Have the students check their reading rates by using the Words per Minute table on pages 154 and 155. They should then enter their reading speed on the Reading Speed graph on page 156. Graphing their reading rates allows the students to keep track of improvement in their reading speed.

**Working Through Each Unit.** If the students have carefully completed all parts of the Sample Unit, they should be ready to tackle the regular units. In each unit, begin by having someone in the class read aloud the introduction to the story, just as you did in the Sample Unit. Discuss the topic of the story, and allow the students time to study the illustration.

Then have the students read the story. If you are timing them, have the students enter their reading time, find their reading speed, and record their speed on the graph after they have finished reading the story.

Next, direct the students to complete the four comprehension exercises *without* looking back at the story. When they have finished, go over the questions and answers with them. The students will grade their own answers and make the necessary corrections. They should then enter their Critical Reading Scores on the graph on page 157.

**The Graphs.** Students enjoy graphing their work. Graphs show, in a concrete and easily understandable way, how a student is progressing. Seeing a line of progressively rising scores gives students the incentive to continue to strive for improvement.

Check the graphs regularly. This will allow you to establish a routine for reviewing each student's progress. Discuss with each student what the graphs show and what kind of progress you expect. Establish guidelines and warning signals so that students will know when to approach you for counseling and advice.

## RELATED TEXTS

If you find that your students enjoy and benefit from the stories and skills exercises in *Apparitions*, you may be interested in *Disasters!, Phenomena, Monsters, Heroes,* and *Eccentrics,* five related Jamestown texts. All feature high-interest stories and work in four critical reading comprehension skills. As in *Apparitions*, the units in those books are divided into three groups, at reading levels six, seven and eight.

SAMPLE UNIT

When West Point cadets started crying Ghost! school officials immediately began an investigation. A number of cadets reported having seen the ghost of a mid-nineteenth-century cavalryman in room 4714. The ghost's uniform, they said, looked like the one on the model shown here. Room 4714 was finally locked and declared off limits. Had someone staged a clever hoax, or was the ghost the real thing? No one knows for sure.

# The West Point Ghost

Cadet Captain Keith W. Bakken did not believe in ghosts. But what other explanation could there be? This was one mystery that had him baffled.

On the night of October 21, 1972, Captain Bakken was asleep in his room at West Point, the U.S. Military Academy on the Hudson River in New York, when a series of loud shouts rudely awakened him. He leaped out of bed and dashed down the hall to room 4714, the source of the shouts. There Captain Bakken found two terrified cadets. "What's going on here?" Captain Bakken demanded. "We've . . . we've seen a . . . a ghost!" the cadets stammered. Then they told their astonishing story.

Both cadets had been sound asleep when they were awakened by a strange noise. At the same time, they felt a chill in the room. Then a ghostly figure floated through the door. Both cadets swore that the figure was a soldier dressed in an old-time uniform. He wore a handlebar mustache and carried a musket.

Cadet Captain Bakken did not know what to make of the eerie tale. Were the men lying? He doubted it. West Point was the oldest military school in the United States, with a fine reputation to uphold. Only the cream of the crop were admitted. Since its founding in 1802, it had produced many of the nation's leaders. In fact,

two presidents were West Point graduates. What's more, all West Point cadets lived by the Honor System. Lying, cheating, or stealing would mean immediate dismissal. No, the two cadets would not risk their careers for the sake of a childish prank. Besides, Captain Bakken thought, they seemed genuinely frightened. And the room *did* feel quite cold.

Wanting to see for himself what was going on, Captain Bakken decided to spend the rest of the night in the room. But the ghost—or whatever it was—did not return.

The next night he asked another cadet to share the room with him. About 2:00 A.M. the ghost returned. Both men saw "a figure partially extended out of the wall," as they later described it. Although it vanished in a short time, the men were sure the ghostly figure wore an old-time uniform. What is more, they agreed that the room had felt "icy-cold."

Word of the ghost soon spread throughout the Point. Soon cadets who had been assigned to room 4714 in past years came forward. They, too, they said, had felt a presence—a ghost—in the room. A trip to the library yielded more information. Uniforms like the one worn by the ghost were standard for soldiers in the 1830s!

The story eventually found its way to the newspapers. "Ghost Haunts West

Point!" screamed the headlines. West Point leaders were upset by the stories. It was not the kind of publicity they wanted for the school. The Point's commanding general declared room 4714 off limits to everyone. All the furniture was removed and the door was padlocked.

As the Christmas holidays drew near, interest in the ghost died down. No more stories appeared in newspapers. Even many of the cadets seemed to forget about it. Then a midshipman from the Point's rival, the U.S. Naval Academy, at Annapolis, Maryland, stepped forward.

The ghost was a Halloween prank, stated Midshipman William Gravell. He confessed to being the one behind the hoax. The "ghost," he said, was nothing more than a picture he had projected on a wall of room 4714. What about the ice-cold room? That was nothing more than carbon dioxide shot from a fire extinguisher, Midshipman Gravell explained. Then he smiled, for he was pleased with himself. The prank, he admitted, had been more successful than he had hoped.

And that ends the story of the West Point ghost. Or does it? Of course, the cadets at the Point hated to think they had been fooled by someone from their rival academy. The ghost had to be real, they said. Too many cadets claimed to have seen the apparition. Besides, there were just too many holes in the midshipman's story. For one thing, the Point in New York and the Naval Academy in Maryland are about four hundred miles apart. How could Gravell have traveled that distance on so many occasions without being missed at school? What's more, how could he have hidden himself and the projector inside room 4714? Surely someone would have seen him. No, the cadets argued, Midshipman Gravell could not have done what he claimed.

*The Pointer,* a student newspaper, offered these possible explanations. About a hundred years ago, a West Point officer died in a house fire. The house stood not far from the site of the 47th Division Barracks—the building in which room 4714 is situated. Perhaps the ghost was that of the dead soldier? Or perhaps it was the ghost of a restless soul from an old burial ground nearby?

The apparition has not reappeared since 1972. Room 4714 was reopened in 1978, and there have been no further reports of the ghostly soldier. So perhaps it was the product of a hoax after all. On the other hand, who was responsible and how did they pull it off? Unless it appears again, we may never know the truth behind the West Point ghost. ■

*If you have been timed while reading this selection, enter your reading time below. Then turn to the Words per Minute table on page 154 and look up your reading speed (words per minute). When you are working through the regular units, you will then enter your reading speed on the graph on page 156.*

READING TIME: Sample Unit

_____ : _____
*Minutes*        *Seconds*

# How well did you read?

- *The four types of questions that follow appear in each unit in this book. The directions for each kind of question tell you how to mark your answers. In this Sample Unit, the answers are marked for you. Also, for the Main Idea and Making Inferences exercises, explanations of the answers are given, to help you understand how to think through these question types. Read through these exercises carefully.*

- *When you have finished all four exercises in a unit, you will check your work by using the answer key that starts on page 150. For each right answer, you will put a check mark (✔) on the line beside the box. For each wrong answer, you will write the correct answer on the line.*

- *For scoring each exercise, you will follow the directions below the questions. In this unit, sample scores are entered as examples.*

## A FINDING THE MAIN IDEA

Look at the three statements below. One expresses the main idea of the story you just read. A good main idea statement answers two questions: it tells *who* or *what* is the subject of the story, and it answers the understood question *does what?* or *is what?* Another statement is *too broad,* it is vague and doesn't tell much about the topic of the story. The third statement is *too narrow,* it tells about only one part of the story.

Match the statements with the three answer choices below by writing the letter of each answer in the box in front of the statement it goes with.

**M—Main Idea**     **B—Too Broad**     **N—Too Narrow**

✔ | B | 1. Strange, unexplained occurrences have taken place at the U.S. Military Academy.

[This statement is true, but it is *too broad.* The story is about particular strange occurrences—the sightings of a ghost.]

✔ | N | 2. The West Point ghost appeared to be the ghost of a soldier from the last century.

[This statement is true, but it is *too narrow.* It gives only one piece of information from the story.]

✔ | M | 3. The reported appearance of a ghostly soldier at West Point in 1972 caused an uproar, and no one has ever been able to determine what caused the apparition.

[This statement is the *main idea.* It tells you what the reading selection is about—a ghost at West Point. It also tells you that the mystery of the ghost was never solved.]

__15__ Score 15 points for a correct *M* answer

__10__ Score 5 points for each correct *B* or *N* answer

__25__ TOTAL SCORE: Finding the Main Idea

## B RECALLING FACTS

How well do you remember the facts in the story you just read? Put an *x* in the box in front of the correct answer to each of the multiple choice questions below.

1. William Gravell was a
   - ✓   ☐ a. captain at West Point.
   -   ☒ b. student at the U.S. Naval Academy.
   -   ☐ c. newspaper reporter.

2. The Honor System requires cadets to
   - ✓   ☒ a. be honest.
   -   ☐ b. respect their superiors.
   -   ☐ c. be brave.

3. Room 4714 was
   - ✓   ☒ a. in the 47th Division Barracks.
   -   ☐ b. on the site of a burial ground.
   -   ☐ c. Captain Bakken's room.

4. Everyone who saw it said that the ghost
   - ✓   ☒ a. carried a musket.
   -   ☐ b. was dressed as a Revolutionary War soldier.
   -   ☐ c. wore a gray uniform.

5. The U.S. Military Academy is located in
   -   ☐ a. California.
   -   ☐ b. Maryland.
   - ✓   ☒ c. New York.

Score 5 points for each correct answer

**25**   TOTAL SCORE: Recalling Facts

## C MAKING INFERENCES

An inference is a judgment that is made or an idea that is arrived at based on facts or on information that is given. You make an inference when you understand something that is *not* stated directly, but that is *implied,* or suggested by the facts that are given.

Below are five statements that are judgments or ideas that have been arrived at from the facts of the story. Write the letter *C* in the box in front of each statement that is a correct inference. Write the letter *F* in front of each faulty inference.

**C—Correct Inference     F—Faulty Inference**

✓   C   1. West Point officials guarded the reputation of the school carefully.
[This is a *correct* inference. You are told in the story that officials at the school were upset by newspaper reports of the ghost, because the stories did not provide the kind of publicity they wanted for the school.]

✓   F   2. Keith Bakken believed that the West Point ghost was a real ghost, not part of a hoax.
[This is a *faulty* inference. There is nothing in the story to indicate whether Captain Bakken believed that the ghost was real or not.]

✓   C   3. The West Point cadets didn't want to believe that the ghost was a hoax created by someone from the Naval Academy.
[This is a *correct* inference. The cadets wouldn't have wanted to admit that someone from their biggest rival had fooled them so effectively.]

✓   F   4. People have given up trying to find out whether the West Point ghost was real or not.
[This is a *faulty* inference. The questions remain unanswered. The fact that stories are being written about it today suggests that many people are still curious about the apparition.]

✓   F   5. Midshipman William Gravell was dismissed from the Naval Academy for confessing to being responsible for the ghost at West Point.
[This is a *faulty* inference. There is nothing in the story to indicate that Midshipman Gravell was punished in any way.]

Score 5 points for each correct answer

**25**   TOTAL SCORE: Making Inferences

# D USING WORDS PRECISELY

Each of the numbered sentences below contains an underlined word or phrase from the story you have just read. Under the sentence are three definitions. One has the *same* meaning as the underlined word or phrase, one has *almost the same* meaning, and one has the *opposite* meaning. Match the definitions with the three answer choices by writing the letter that stands for each answer in the box in front of the definition it goes with.

S—Same    A—Almost the Same    O—Opposite

1. "We've . . . we've seen a . . . a ghost!" the cadets <u>stammered</u>.

   ✓ [A] a. jabbered

   ✓ [S] b. said falteringly

   ✓ [O] c. stated clearly

2. Cadet Captain Bakken did not know what to make of the <u>eerie</u> tale.

   ✓ [A] a. odd

   ✓ [S] b. weird

   ✓ [O] c. sensible

3. Besides, Captain Bakken thought, they seemed <u>genuinely</u> frightened.

   ✓ [S] a. truly

   ✓ [A] b. obviously

   ✓ [O] c. falsely

4. A trip to the library <u>yielded</u> more information.

   ✓ [S] a. produced

   ✓ [O] b. used up

   ✓ [A] c. uncovered

5. Then a midshipman from the Point's <u>rival</u>, the U.S. Naval Academy, at Annapolis, Maryland, stepped forward.

   ✓ [O] a. partner

   ✓ [A] b. enemy

   ✓ [S] c. competitor

   __15__ Score 3 points for each correct *S* answer
   __10__ Score 1 point for each correct *A* or *O* answer
   __25__ TOTAL SCORE: Using Words Precisely

● *Enter the four total scores in the spaces below, and add them together to find your Critical Reading Score. Then record your Critical Reading Score on the graph on page 157.*

| | |
|---|---|
| _____ | Finding the Main Idea |
| _____ | Recalling Facts |
| _____ | Making Inferences |
| _____ | Using Words Precisely |
| _____ | CRITICAL READING SCORE: Sample Unit |

# To the Student

Stories of ghosts may send tingles up our spines, but we still
love to hear them. You've probably found spooky stories
fascinating yourself, even if they scare you. Ghost stories have
probably been around as long as people have. Why do they hold
our interest so strongly? Perhaps it is because we wonder if it
is really possible for the dead to communicate with the living,
or to come back in some form. Maybe we wonder if we ourselves
could appear as ghosts someday. Is there an invisible world outside this one?

This book brings you twenty-two tales of apparitions—
unexplainable appearances of beings or things. We have
stretched the definition of *apparitions* to include unexplainable
voices or sounds, as well as strange sightings, because some
mighty unusual happenings have had no visible explanations.
Some of the tales in the book have been around for hundreds of
years, others are quite fresh. Our stories poke and prod the tales
to try to get to the truth, but that's not always easy—or possible.
In some cases, you'll just have to make up your own mind.

While you are enjoying these fascinating stories, you will be
developing your reading skills. This book assumes that you
already are a fairly good reader. *Apparitions* is for students who
want to read faster and to increase their understanding of what
they read. If you complete all twenty-one units—reading the
stories and completing the exercises—you will surely improve
both your reading rate and your comprehension.

# GROUP ONE

# The Bell Witch

"Ouch!" Twelve-year-old Betsy Bell put her hand to her face. "Stop it!" she screamed, jumping in pain. Both Betsy's cheeks were flaming, as if someone had slapped her across the face. But who—or what—could have done the slapping? That was the mystery. For Betsy was all alone in the room.

It was not the first time Betsy had been hurt by an invisible attacker. For several weeks, she and other members of the Bell family had been tormented. Their beds were torn apart. Their hair was pulled, their noses were pinched, and their faces were slapped.

"The blows were distinctly heard," Betsy's brother Williams later wrote, "like the open palm of a heavy hand." Thanks to Williams Bell, we have a firsthand account of the strange happenings in the Bell household. Although he was only six when they began, years later he wrote an account of the events.

According to Williams, the trouble started in 1817, on a warm Indian summer's night in Tennessee. John Bell and his wife, Lucy, and their eight children had finished supper. Then, as was their custom, they gathered around the hearth. John Bell, a staunch Baptist, liked to read to the family from the Bible. But on this night, loud rapping and scraping noises interrupted his reading. John Bell glared at his children. "Quiet!" he said sternly. "This is no time for pranks."

The children looked up at him innocently. "We did nothing, Father," said Joel. John Bell tried to continue his reading, but the noises persisted. Now he truly looked angry. "Really, Father," said John, Jr., "the noises are coming from outside." The boy was right. It was as if someone was clawing at the doors and windows of the house, trying to get in.

After that, the noises were heard every night. Soon they moved indoors. There were sounds of rats gnawing on wood and of a dog's claws scraping across the floor. Wood seemed to crack and splinter, as if the beds were being torn apart. Then the noises became human. Strangling and choking sounds seemed to come from everywhere. But although the Bells searched the house from top to bottom, they could find nothing amiss.

The Bells kept their problem a secret for almost a year. John Bell was a respected farmer, and he was afraid people would think he was crazy if he told what was going on. But when his children were attacked, he decided to get help. He invited James Johnson, a neighbor who was a lay preacher, to the farm.

Astonished at the sounds he heard, Johnson was convinced that an evil spirit was at work. "Stop, I beseech you, in the name of the Lord!" he commanded. To everyone's surprise, the noises did stop. But they soon started again, even louder than before. In fact, they were so loud that they fairly shook the house. What is more, the attacks on the Bells became even more vicious.

By that time, news of the strange happenings at the Bell farm had spread throughout Robertson County. Every night the house filled with people who wanted to hear the noises for themselves. They were not disappointed. The source of the noises remained invisible, but along with the sounds, soft whispers began to be heard. At first the words were difficult to understand. Then, gradually, whole sentences became clear.

Of course, now that the presence could speak, listeners asked it to explain who or what it was. A number of answers were given.

"I am a spirit from everywhere—heaven, hell, the earth," the voice said. "I am in the air, in houses—any place at any time. I have been created for millions of years." Another time it said, "I am a spirit. I was once very happy, but I have been disturbed."

The spirit told its audience a number of wild tales. But the story that most interested people concerned a local woman who was thought by many people to be a witch. "I am the spirit of old Kate Batts," said the voice one evening.

Kate Batts had once done business with John Bell. Claiming afterward that Bell had cheated her, Kate vowed revenge. "I'll get him!" she swore to all who would listen. But the townspeople were used to Kate's evil tongue. She was stubborn and bad-tempered. As a result, she had many enemies. People loved the idea that the spirit claimed to be that of old Kate. It did not matter that the woman was still alive. From then on, the spirit was referred to as Kate, The Bell Witch.

Not everyone believed in the spirit, though. Since most of the violence was directed at Betsy, it was suggested that she might be causing the problem. Betsy was accused of ventriloquism, or "throwing her voice." John, Jr., suggested a test to see if this was true. He asked a visiting doctor to place his hand over Betsy's mouth at a time when the voice was speaking. The doctor did, and he declared that Betsy certainly was not making the sounds.

There was other proof of Betsy's innocence. Hoping to spare her further torture from the spirit, the Bells sent Betsy to live with neighbors. But there, too, she was tormented. And while she was away, the

Bell household continued to be attacked. There was no way Betsy could have caused the occurrences at the farm. But a spirit could easily manage to trouble two places, said believers.

At some point the Bell Witch tired of Betsy and turned its attentions to John Bell. Bell's tongue grew stiff and swollen, so he could neither eat nor speak for hours. The spirit seemed to enjoy John Bell's suffering. "I will torment you into your grave!" she threatened.

Kate's nature was not all evil, however. She loved to quote from the Bible. When ministers visited the Bell farm, she would

*The Bell Witch is so much a part of the history of Robertson County, Tennessee, that the Tennessee Historical Commission has erected a roadside marker telling about her. When the spirit arrived, it focused its attention on the unfortunate Bell family, who lived in a big log cabin situated in the field shown above, where the large tree on the right now stands. The cabin is gone, but is the witch?*

talk with them at length. She prayed and even sang hymns. Those who heard her said she had a charming voice.

At times Kate even made herself useful. One night Lucy Bell wondered aloud whether her son Jesse had yet returned from a trip. "Wait a minute, Luce. I'll go and see for you," said Kate. A few seconds later, she returned with a report. "He's home," she said. "He's sitting at a table reading by the light of a candle." Jesse, who lived a mile away, later confirmed Kate's report.

Lucy Bell was a favorite of Kate's. When Lucy became ill, the spirit brought her gifts. She cracked nuts and dropped them onto the bed. She brought oranges, bananas, and grapes—fruits that in those days could not be found in Tennessee. Kate claimed she had gotten them in the West Indies.

About that time, Betsy Bell fell in love with a young man named Joshua Gardner. The Bells were delighted with the match. Kate, however, was not. "Betsy Bell," she said, "do not marry Joshua Gardner." At first the spirit pleaded sweetly. But when Betsy ignored the warnings, Kate grew furious. She did everything she could to break up their romance.

Kate also began a serious attack on John Bell, whom she called "Old Jack." The poor man became very ill. The doctors could find no cure. Finally, on December 19, 1820, Williams found his father in a coma. By his side was a vial of strange-looking liquid. When it was tested on the family cat, the animal died almost at once. Their worst fears were realized: poison.

"I put it there!" cried Kate. "I gave Old Jack a big dose of it last night while he was asleep, which fixed him." John Bell died the next morning, as Kate shouted and sang with glee. She had made good on her threat to torment John Bell to his grave.

For a while after John Bell's death, the spirit visited less often. The Bells began to think that life might return to normal. But when Betsy and Joshua became engaged, Kate again plagued the couple. She said so many horrid things to them in front of their friends that they were embarrassed to be seen in public. Finally Betsy had had enough. She broke her engagement.

This seemed to satisfy Kate, for that spring she announced that she was leaving. Before she left, however, she made one more threat. "Good-bye," she called out, "I leave for now. But I will return in seven years." With that, something like a cannon ball rolled down the chimney and burst into smoke. Kate had plagued the Bell family for four long years. At last, they were once again at peace.

Seven years later, however, the spirit kept her promise. She returned to the Bell farm and for two weeks scratched at the doors and windows. Needless to say, the Bells were terrified. Luckily, Kate never entered the house. However, she did visit the home of John Bell, Jr., who had married and started a family of his own. She had a message to deliver. "I will be back in 107 years!" she declared. Then she left.

Well, 107 years have come and gone. So far Kate has not made another grand appearance at the Bell farm. But the people of Robertson County swear that she never left. Strange, unexplainable occurrences continue to this day. Many of them center around a cave at the edge of the Bell farm. People have reported seeing the figure of a woman floating through the cave. Some say they have been touched by something invisible. Footsteps and the sound of dragging chains have been heard. And in surrounding fields, odd floating lights are sometimes seen. If someone tries to approach them, they disappear and then reappear in another spot. The Bell Witch is pretty much an accepted resident of the area. Whenever something unusual happens, folks just shrug and say, "Kate probably did it." ■

*If you have been timed while reading this selection, enter your reading time below. Then turn to the Words per Minute table on page 154 and look up your reading speed (words per minute). Enter your reading speed on the graph on page 156.*

READING TIME: Unit 1

_____ : _____
*Minutes*      *Seconds*

# How well did you read?

- *Answer the four types of questions that follow. The directions for each type of question tell you how to mark your answers.*

- *When you have finished all four exercises, check your work by using the answer key on page 150. For each right answer, put a check mark (✔) on the line beside the box. For each wrong answer, write the correct answer on the line.*

- *For scoring each exercise, follow the directions below the questions.*

## A FINDING THE MAIN IDEA

Look at the three statements below. One expresses the main idea of the story you just read. A good main idea statement answers two questions: it tells *who* or *what* is the subject of the story, and it answers the understood question *does what?* or *is what?* Another statement is *too broad,* it is vague and doesn't tell much about the topic of the story. The third statement is *too narrow,* it tells about only one part of the story.

Match the statements with the three answer choices below by writing the letter of each answer in the box in front of the statement it goes with.

**M—Main Idea**     **B—Too Broad**     **N—Too Narrow**

_____ ☐ 1. Kate tormented John Bell to his grave.

_____ ☐ 2. The Bell family was tormented for years by a wicked spirit known as Kate.

_____ ☐ 3. The Bell family were victims of seemingly supernatural occurrences.

_____ Score 15 points for a correct *M* answer

_____ Score 5 points for each correct *B* or *N* answer

_____ TOTAL SCORE: Finding the Main Idea

## B RECALLING FACTS

How well do you remember the facts in the story you just read? Put an *x* in the box in front of the correct answer to each of the multiple choice questions below.

1. The story of The Bell Witch takes place in
   - ___ ☐ a. Georgia.
   - ___ ☐ b. South Carolina.
   - ___ ☐ c. Tennessee.

2. John Bell and his wife, Lucy, had
   - ___ ☐ a. two children.
   - ___ ☐ b. six children.
   - ___ ☐ c. eight children.

3. John Bell was a
   - ___ ☐ a. farmer.
   - ___ ☐ b. lay preacher.
   - ___ ☐ c. doctor.

4. Kate Batts was
   - ___ ☐ a. John Bell's sister.
   - ___ ☐ b. a woman John Bell had once done business with.
   - ___ ☐ c. James Johnson's wife.

5. When the spirit left the second time, it promised that it would return in
   - ___ ☐ a. 7 years.
   - ___ ☐ b. 100 years.
   - ___ ☐ c. 107 years.

Score 5 points for each correct answer

___ TOTAL SCORE: Recalling Facts

## C MAKING INFERENCES

An inference is a judgment that is made or an idea that is arrived at based on facts or on information that is given. You make an inference when you understand something that is *not* stated directly, but that is *implied,* or suggested by the facts that are given.

Below are five statements that are judgments or ideas that have been arrived at from the facts of the story. Write the letter *C* in the box in front of each statement that is a correct inference. Write the letter *F* in front of each faulty inference.

**C—Correct Inference     F—Faulty Inference**

- ___ ☐ 1. Williams Bell thought the spirit was a hoax.

- ___ ☐ 2. Betsy Bell never married.

- ___ ☐ 3. Kate Batts lied when she said that John Bell had cheated her.

- ___ ☐ 4. The spirit made a strong impression on Williams Bell.

- ___ ☐ 5. The Bells' neighbors were not afraid of the spirit.

Score 5 points for each correct answer

___ TOTAL SCORE: Making Inferences

## D USING WORDS PRECISELY

Each of the numbered sentences below contains an underlined word or phrase from the story you have just read. Under the sentence are three definitions. One has the *same* meaning as the underlined word or phrase, one has *almost the same* meaning, and one has the *opposite* meaning. Match the definitions with the three answer choices by writing the letter that stands for each answer in the box in front of the definition it goes with.

**S—Same    A—Almost the Same    O—Opposite**

1. "The blows were distinctly heard," Betsy's brother Williams later wrote.

   ____ ☐ a. strongly

   ____ ☐ b. clearly

   ____ ☐ c. vaguely

2. John Bell, a staunch Baptist, liked to read to the family from the Bible.

   ____ ☐ a. strict

   ____ ☐ b. faithful

   ____ ☐ c. careless

3. John Bell tried to continue his reading, but the noises persisted.

   ____ ☐ a. stopped

   ____ ☐ b. continued

   ____ ☐ c. remained

4. But although the Bells searched the house from top to bottom, they could find nothing amiss.

   ____ ☐ a. right

   ____ ☐ b. inappropriate

   ____ ☐ c. wrong

5. Jesse, who lived a mile away, later confirmed Kate's report.

   ____ ☐ a. proved

   ____ ☐ b. denied

   ____ ☐ c. verified

____ Score 3 points for each correct S answer
____ Score 1 point for each correct A or O answer

____ TOTAL SCORE: Using Words Precisely

● *Enter the four total scores in the spaces below, and add them together to find your Critical Reading Score. Then record your Critical Reading Score on the graph on page 157.*

____ Finding the Main Idea
____ Recalling Facts
____ Making Inferences
____ Using Words Precisely
____ CRITICAL READING SCORE: Unit 1

The Gray Man has been a valuable friend to the people on Pawley's Island for a long time. He doesn't show up often, but when he does, people pay attention. Though he seems shy and is short on words, his appearance carries a big message: get off the island—fast. Those who are wise take that message seriously, for they know that the Gray Man is not a fair-weather friend.

# The Gray Man of Pawley's Island

The Gray Man is no ordinary ghost. In fact, to the people who live on Pawley's Island, South Carolina, he is a hero. It is said that he has saved thousands of lives.

The Gray Man hardly looks like a champion, however. He is short and skinny. He dresses in odd-looking clothes—a gray suit with a long jacket, and a hat shaped like a turtle shell. He does have one remarkable feature, though—he is faceless. The Gray Man has no eyes, no nose, no mouth.

The Gray Man has been seen walking in the surf on the edge of Pawley's Island. He has also been spotted sitting on top of a sand dune staring out to sea, and wandering among swimmers and sunbathers on the beach. But islanders claim that whenever someone has given him a second look, he has instantly vanished.

Who is the Gray Man, and why does he appear on Pawley's Island? According to the islanders, the Gray Man materializes only before bad storms. His appearance gives warning of the storm. Islanders do not take those warnings lightly. They swear he has yet to be wrong. What is more, they say, whoever sees the Gray Man is spared by the storm.

Little Mary McLendon was one of those lucky people. Mary first visited Pawley's Island when she was nine years old. She stayed with her grandmother, who had a house there. A few days before the end of her vacation, Mary took a long walk along the beach. It was late afternoon. Suddenly, ahead of her on a dune, she saw a figure that she recognized as the Gray Man. As she ran to catch up to him, he grew dim and faded away. Mary turned and scurried to her grandmother's house.

"Granny! Granny!" she cried, "I have seen the Gray Man. There will be a storm! We must leave the island! Quick, Granny, hurry!"

At the same time, a neighbor rushed up to say that a hurricane was indeed on the way. Mary and her grandmother quickly packed and left the island for the town of Georgetown, where Mrs. McLendon had another home.

That night the storm struck Pawley's. It dumped several inches of rain and swept the island with a terrible destruction. In the calm that followed, Mary and her grandmother returned. Everywhere, it seemed, houses had been swept away and palm trees uprooted. Except for at the McLendon's. The property was untouched. A doll's suitcase Mary had forgotten on the front step was still there. Clothes that had been hung on a line remained neatly in place. It was as if a giant protective bubble had been lowered over the house while the storm raged all around.

Other islanders have had similar experiences. No wonder, then, that they insist that the Gray Man exists. But who was, or is, he? There are several theories.

Some folks think he is the ghost of Percival Pawley, the first settler of Pawley's Island. Others, however, claim he is the ghost of a young man who lived in the eighteenth century—a man who was to have married the daughter of a rich plantation owner.

The man and woman, it is said, were cousins. They had been separated for two years when the young man was killed in a duel in Europe. Hearing of his death, his fiancée retreated to her room, vowing to stay there until her own life should end.

Then one day an old friend paid her a call. He had recently lost his wife, so the two had something in common to talk about. Their conversations led to a renewed friendship, and eventually to love and marriage. The couple went to live in Charleston, South Carolina. They also kept a home on Pawley's Island, where they spent the summers.

Then came the summer of 1778. It was the midst of the American Revolution. The woman went to live on Pawley's while her husband fought the British. Late in the summer, a hurricane struck.

Fortunately for the young woman, her home was unharmed. In the calm after the storm, a survivor from a shipwreck knocked at her door, seeking help. When the woman opened the door, whom should she see standing there but the cousin who had supposedly been killed in a duel! She fainted with shock, and the shipwrecked man fled. He was found on the mainland a few days later, dead of some kind of fever.

After the revolution, the woman and her husband were reunited. They continued to spend summers on Pawley's. But wherever she was on the island, the woman was haunted by a shadowy figure that followed her at a distance. She was sure it was the ghost of her cousin.

Within months, other residents of the island began to talk of a gray figure that appeared just before storms. Over the years that followed, he appeared before all of the fiercest storms. The Gray Man was seen just before the great storms of 1822, 1893, and 1916 shattered the island. He was seen again in 1954, just before Hurricane Hazel hit. And he was there again a year later, when Hurricane Connie devastated the entire Carolina coast.

Each time, all who saw him, and all who believed the warnings of those people, had ample time to leave the island. Their lives were spared. As for the fate of those who either didn't see the Gray Man or didn't believe in his warnings, you have only to look at photographs showing the awful destruction on Pawley's Island after those storms. ■

*If you have been timed while reading this selection, enter your reading time below. Then turn to the Words per Minute table on page 154 and look up your reading speed (words per minute). Enter your reading speed on the graph on page 156.*

| READING TIME: Unit 2 |
|---|
| _____ : _____ |
| *Minutes*      *Seconds* |

# How well did you read?

- *Answer the four types of questions that follow. The directions for each type of question tell you how to mark your answers.*

- *When you have finished all four exercises, check your work by using the answer key on page 150. For each right answer, put a check mark (✔) on the line beside the box. For each wrong answer, write the correct answer on the line.*

- *For scoring each exercise, follow the directions below the questions.*

## A FINDING THE MAIN IDEA

Look at the three statements below. One expresses the main idea of the story you just read. A good main idea statement answers two questions: it tells *who* or *what* is the subject of the story, and it answers the understood question *does what?* or *is what?* Another statement is *too broad,* it is vague and doesn't tell much about the topic of the story. The third statement is *too narrow,* it tells about only one part of the story.

Match the statements with the three answer choices below by writing the letter of each answer in the box in front of the statement it goes with.

**M—Main Idea**     **B—Too Broad**     **N—Too Narrow**

_____ ☐ 1. A ghost called the Gray Man is said to appear on Pawley's Island, South Carolina, to warn people of approaching storms.

_____ ☐ 2. The Gray Man of Pawley's Island is a ghost.

_____ ☐ 3. Pawley's Island, South Carolina, has a resident ghost that helps the islanders.

_____ Score 15 points for a correct *M* answer

_____ Score 5 points for each correct *B* or *N* answer

_____ TOTAL SCORE: Finding the Main Idea

27

## B RECALLING FACTS

How well do you remember the facts in the story you just read?
Put an *x* in the box in front of the correct answer to each of the
multiple choice questions below.

1. The Gray Man
   ____ ☐ a. never appears in winter.
   ____ ☐ b. has no face.
   ____ ☐ c. is the ghost of a British soldier.

2. When Mary McLendon saw the Gray Man, she
   ____ ☐ a. had just settled on the island.
   ____ ☐ b. was sick with a fever.
   ____ ☐ c. was nine years old.

3. The cousin of the plantation owner's daughter was
   killed in
   ____ ☐ a. the Revolutionary War.
   ____ ☐ b. a duel.
   ____ ☐ c. a storm at sea.

4. According to the story, the Gray Man has been
   around for
   ____ ☐ a. about two hundred years.
   ____ ☐ b. about a hundred years.
   ____ ☐ c. almost four hundred years.

5. The Gray Man is
   ____ ☐ a. tall and skinny.
   ____ ☐ b. short and fat.
   ____ ☐ c. short and skinny.

Score 5 points for each correct answer

____ TOTAL SCORE: Recalling Facts

## C MAKING INFERENCES

An inference is a judgment that is made or an idea that is
arrived at based on facts or on information that is given. You
make an inference when you understand something that is *not*
stated directly, but that is *implied*, or suggested by the facts that
are given.

Below are five statements that are judgments or ideas that
have been arrived at from the facts of the story. Write the letter
*C* in the box in front of each statement that is a correct inference. Write the letter *F* in front of each faulty inference.

**C—Correct Inference      F—Faulty Inference**

____ ☐ 1. The Gray Man has never spoken to anyone.

____ ☐ 2. Pawley's Island is a summer vacation spot.

____ ☐ 3. The Gray Man has not been seen since Hurricane
         Connie, in 1955.

____ ☐ 4. Mary McLendon was frightened at the sight of
         the Gray Man.

____ ☐ 5. The residents of Pawley's Island like having a
         ghost around.

Score 5 points for each correct answer

____ TOTAL SCORE: Making Inferences

## D USING WORDS PRECISELY

Each of the numbered sentences below contains an underlined word or phrase from the story you have just read. Under the sentence are three definitions. One has the *same* meaning as the underlined word or phrase, one has *almost the same* meaning, and one has the *opposite* meaning. Match the definitions with the three answer choices by writing the letter that stands for each answer in the box in front of the definition it goes with.

**S—Same      A—Almost the Same      O—Opposite**

1. He does have one <u>remarkable</u> feature.

   ____  ☐ a. extraordinary

   ____  ☐ b. common

   ____  ☐ c. odd

2. According to the islanders, the Gray Man <u>materializes</u> only before bad storms.

   ____  ☐ a. happens

   ____  ☐ b. vanishes

   ____  ☐ c. appears

3. Their conversations led to a <u>renewed</u> friendship, and eventually to love and marriage.

   ____  ☐ a. reestablished

   ____  ☐ b. continued

   ____  ☐ c. ended

4. Each time, all who saw him, and all who believed the warnings of those people, had <u>ample</u> time to leave the island.

   ____  ☐ a. enough

   ____  ☐ b. plenty

   ____  ☐ c. too little

5. As for the <u>fate</u> of those who didn't believe in the warnings, you have only to look at photographs showing the awful destruction on Pawley's Island after those storms.

   ____  ☐ a. doom

   ____  ☐ b. start

   ____  ☐ c. final outcome

____ Score 3 points for each correct *S* answer
____ Score 1 point for each correct *A* or *O* answer

____ TOTAL SCORE: Using Words Precisely

- *Enter the four total scores in the spaces below, and add them together to find your Critical Reading Score. Then record your Critical Reading Score on the graph on page 157.*

  _____ Finding the Main Idea
  _____ Recalling Facts
  _____ Making Inferences
  _____ Using Words Precisely

  _____ CRITICAL READING SCORE: Unit 2

Sailors have long met in ports around the world to socialize and exchange tales of their voyages—to talk of storms at sea, of exotic places they have been, and of strange and exciting things they have seen. For centuries, there was one story that was told over and over again (varying a bit depending on who was doing the telling). The main character was always the same: a ghostly sailing ship. And the warning at the end of the tale never varied: if you see the Flying Dutchman, stay away from it.

# The Flying Dutchman

Five hundred years ago a merchant ship set sail from some long forgotten port. Its destination, also long forgotten, lay beyond the Cape of Good Hope, off the southern tip of Africa. In command of the vessel was a Dutch seafarer named Bernard Fokke.

Captain Fokke had a reputation as a fearless (some might say reckless) sailor. Indeed, he regularly ventured out to sea in weather that kept other captains in port. He liked to sail where the winds were strong enough to, in his own words, "blow the horns off a bull." To cope with such violent weather, he had the wooden masts of his ship encased in iron. That allowed him to carry more sail without the masts snapping from the great pressure of the winds.

In addition to being fearless, Bernard Fokke was a cruel and jealous man. He was given to uncontrollable rages. On the eve of his wedding day, for example, he murdered his wife-to-be and his own brother. He had become insanely jealous when he caught the two talking together. Fokke's violent personality was to prove his downfall.

The voyage with which this tale concerns itself took place shortly after the murders. All went well until the ship reached the Cape of Good Hope. Then the Cape lived up to its other name—the Cape of Storms. Captain Fokke and his crew sailed into gale force winds and mountainous waves. It was Fokke's kind of weather.

Within hours the vessel was staggering under the constant battering of wind and waves. One of the three masts snapped. Virtually every sail was in tatters.

Standing in his accustomed place beside the wheel, Captain Fokke remained the picture of serenity. He was actually smiling as he puffed on his pipe. The storm provided the kind of challenge he relished.

His crew, however, were terrified. "We are doomed!" they cried. "We must turn back, we must!" "Never!" came Captain Fokke's reply. "There is no storm—there is *nothing*—that can harm me. I will not turn back!"

Hearing those words, the crew deserted their posts and fell to their knees in prayer. There they stayed, despite Fokke's shouts of protest. His anger had escalated to wrath when suddenly a sailor lunged at him, grasped him by the arm, and pleaded, "Turn back, Captain! For God's sake, turn back!"

Captain Fokke had had enough of such talk. He picked the man up and flung him into the sea. "May you suffer the death of a coward!" he shouted as the man slipped beneath the waves.

Here the line between history and legend blurs. The stories say that at that moment the storm clouds parted and a strange figure took shape on deck. The crew, still on their knees, grew more terrified than ever. Captain Fokke calmly relit his pipe and turned his back.

"Captain Fokke," said the apparition, "you are a cruel man, an evil man." At that, Fokke turned and, in a mocking voice, replied, "I did not ask your opinion, spirit, or whoever you are." He drew his pistol and added, "Get off my ship, or I shall blow your head off." When the figure showed no sign of leaving, Fokke raised his pistol and fired. Rather than striking the figure, however, the bullet ripped through the captain's own hand. He let out a howl of rage and leaped to strike the figure, only to find that he could not raise his arm. It lay paralyzed at his side.

Captain Fokke shouted a stream of insults and curses at the apparition. At that outburst, the inhuman figure drew itself up until it towered over Fokke and his ship. "It is you who are cursed," it announced. "Mark you my words, Captain Fokke. You shall sail on forever. You shall never rest, nor shall you see port of any kind. You shall be forced to drink gall, and red-hot iron shall be your food. Your crew will grow horns and have the faces of tigers, and their skin shall be that of the dogfish."

That was too much even for Captain Fokke, who took to groaning in anguish at the curse. The members of his crew faded away. In their places appeared the horrible creatures the apparition had described.

Then the mysterious figure continued. "You shall never rest, Captain Fokke. A sword shall pierce your body should you ever close your eyes. And since it is your delight to torment sailors, you shall do so. All the sailors of the sea will tremble at your name." Hearing those words, Captain Fokke felt buoyed. "Ah," he mused, "that is good. Yes, that is indeed good."

The figure then uttered these closing words: "Your ship will bring misfortune to all who see it, and you will be forced to sail for all eternity." Then the visitor vanished.

As the enormity of the curse sank in, the smile disappeared from Captain Fokke's face, and he began groaning again. By that time his ship had turned a ghostly gray. It flew a pale flag and moved under the power of many-colored sails. It took up its endless voyage in search of unsuspecting ships whose sailors it could torment.

Over time, in ports all over the world, stories of a ghostly vessel spread among sailors. Many claimed to have met it on the high seas, or to have heard of ships that had. All warned against having anything to do with the strange vessel, which had come to be called the Flying Dutchman. Reports of encounters with the Dutchman varied. According to some, it would lure ships into dangerous waters where they would wreck themselves on the shoals. Others said that it would take the shape of a friendly vessel whose crew would deliver long-awaited letters to sailors on board a ship. Any sailors who read the letters, however, were doomed. They and their ship would soon be lost in a violent storm.

So grew the legends of the Flying Dutchman. Seamen came to believe that it was the hell of sailors. Cruel or cowardly sailors, it was said, would be condemned for eternity to be part of the awful crew of that ghastly ship. Together with the evil Captain Fokke, they would sail forever, never resting, never touching land.

The Flying Dutchman is the most famous ghost ship of all. Poems have been written about it. Entire books—even an opera—have been written about it. For hundreds of years, sailors were convinced of its existence. Early letters, journals, and ships' logs contain mention after mention of it. Those writings disclose the terror that sailors felt at meeting the ghost ship at sea.

For modern-day sailors, though, the fear is gone. Few any longer believe in the Flying Dutchman. It has become something of a sailing myth. There have been no reported sightings of the ghost ship in more than fifty years. Does that mean that it never really existed? Was it all in the minds of sailors who had been too long at sea? Maybe. But sightings were reported for centuries. And the stories that were told in different parts of the world were strikingly similar.

Some people think the reason for the Flying Dutchman's disappearance lies in one of the many versions of the story. It allows for the possibility that Captain Fokke found a way out of his own sailor's hell.

According to that account, the apparition eventually reappeared to Captain Fokke. "Every seven years," it said to him, "you will take your ship into a different port. There you will walk the streets in search of a woman who will promise to love you until death. If you find such a woman, my curse will be lifted and your soul will rest in peace." ∎

*If you have been timed while reading this selection, enter your reading time below. Then turn to the Words per Minute table on page 154 and look up your reading speed (words per minute). Enter your reading speed on the graph on page 156.*

| READING TIME: Unit 3 | |
|---|---|
| _____ : _____ | |
| *Minutes* | *Seconds* |

# How well did you read?

- *Answer the four types of questions that follow. The directions for each type of question tell you how to mark your answers.*

- *When you have finished all four exercises, check your work by using the answer key on page 150. For each right answer, put a check mark (✔) on the line beside the box. For each wrong answer, write the correct answer on the line.*

- *For scoring each exercise, follow the directions below the questions.*

## A  FINDING THE MAIN IDEA

Look at the three statements below. One expresses the main idea of the story you just read. A good main idea statement answers two questions: it tells *who* or *what* is the subject of the story, and it answers the understood question *does what?* or *is what?* Another statement is *too broad*, it is vague and doesn't tell much about the topic of the story. The third statement is *too narrow*, it tells about only one part of the story.

Match the statements with the three answer choices below by writing the letter of each answer in the box in front of the statement it goes with.

**M—Main Idea**     **B—Too Broad**     **N—Too Narrow**

____  ☐  1. The Flying Dutchman is a ghost ship.

____  ☐  2. A fearsome ghost ship has existed for centuries in the legends of sailors the world over.

____  ☐  3. The Flying Dutchman, according to sailors' legends, is a dreadful ghost ship that lured sailors to their doom.

____  Score 15 points for a correct *M* answer

____  Score 5 points for each correct *B* or *N* answer

____  TOTAL SCORE: Finding the Main Idea

## B RECALLING FACTS

How well do you remember the facts in the story you just read? Put an x in the box in front of the correct answer to each of the multiple choice questions below.

1. Bernard Fokke was
   - ☐ a. African.
   - ☐ b. Dutch.
   - ☐ c. English.

2. One version of the legend said that Fokke would be released from the curse if he
   - ☐ a. saved some sailors.
   - ☐ b. begged forgiveness of the apparition.
   - ☐ c. met a woman who would love him.

3. His ship was bound for
   - ☐ a. the Cape of Good Hope.
   - ☐ b. Cape Horn.
   - ☐ c. somewhere off the southern tip of Africa.

4. As Captain Fokke ordered the spirit to get off his ship he
   - ☐ a. shot at it.
   - ☐ b. tried to stab it with his sword.
   - ☐ c. threw a man overboard.

5. The ghost crew of the Flying Dutchman had faces like
   - ☐ a. dogs.
   - ☐ b. tigers.
   - ☐ c. dogfish.

Score 5 points for each correct answer

_____ TOTAL SCORE: Recalling Facts

## C MAKING INFERENCES

An inference is a judgment that is made or an idea that is arrived at based on facts or on information that is given. You make an inference when you understand something that is *not* stated directly, but that is *implied*, or suggested by the facts that are given.

Below are five statements that are judgments or ideas that have been arrived at from the facts of the story. Write the letter *C* in the box in front of each statement that is a correct inference. Write the letter *F* in front of each faulty inference.

**C—Correct Inference     F—Faulty Inference**

_____ ☐ 1. Bernard Fokke had no regard for human life.

_____ ☐ 2. Fierce storms are common off the Cape of Good Hope.

_____ ☐ 3. Fokke liked having people fear him.

_____ ☐ 4. The sailor who attacked Captain Fokke for not turning back was a coward.

_____ ☐ 5. Fokke's crew trusted Captain Fokke's skills as a sailor.

Score 5 points for each correct answer

_____ TOTAL SCORE: Making Inferences

## D USING WORDS PRECISELY

Each of the numbered sentences below contains an underlined word or phrase from the story you have just read. Under the sentence are three definitions. One has the *same* meaning as the underlined word or phrase, one has *almost the same* meaning, and one has the *opposite* meaning. Match the definitions with the three answer choices by writing the letter that stands for each answer in the box in front of the definition it goes with.

**S—Same     A—Almost the Same     O—Opposite**

1. Standing in his accustomed place beside the wheel, Captain Fokke remained the picture of serenity.

____ ☐ a. self-confidence

____ ☐ b. calmness

____ ☐ c. uneasiness

2. The storm provided the kind of challenge he relished.

____ ☐ a. loved

____ ☐ b. detested

____ ☐ c. welcomed

3. His anger had escalated to wrath when suddenly a sailor lunged at him, grasped him by the arm, and pleaded, "Turn back, Captain!"

____ ☐ a. fell back from

____ ☐ b. pushed

____ ☐ c. rushed forward

4. As the enormity of the curse sank in, the smile disappeared from Captain Fokke's face, and he began groaning again.

____ ☐ a. severeness

____ ☐ b. monstrousness

____ ☐ c. gentleness

5. Those writings disclose the terror that sailors felt at meeting the ghost ship at sea.

____ ☐ a. reveal

____ ☐ b. report

____ ☐ c. hide

____ Score 3 points for each correct S answer
____ Score 1 point for each correct A or O answer

____ TOTAL SCORE: Using Words Precisely

● *Enter the four total scores in the spaces below, and add them together to find your Critical Reading Score. Then record your Critical Reading Score on the graph on page 157.*

____ Finding the Main Idea
____ Recalling Facts
____ Making Inferences
____ Using Words Precisely

____ CRITICAL READING SCORE: Unit 3

*Some strange things happened aboard Eastern Airlines L-1011 Tristar jets after Flight 401 went down. The airline didn't want to admit to ghosts—it didn't even want to discuss them. Spirits weren't exactly good for business. But flight crews and attendants on the planes were having some unsettling experiences for which there seemed to be no other explanation.*

# The Ghosts of Flight 401

It was mid-December 1972. Eastern Airlines flight attendant Doris Elliot was working a flight from New York to Florida when she suddenly got what she later described as a "weird, sick feeling." In her mind she saw a vision of an Eastern jet flying at night over the Florida Everglades. The left wing of the plane crumpled, and the jet hurtled into the swamp. Screams pierced the night.

White as a sheet, Doris fell into a seat. Two other attendants asked her what was wrong. Doris told them what she had "seen." It was not her first experience with such visions. She had often had mental pictures of events that later took place in real life.

The two attendants were shaken. They had faith in Doris's premonitions. "When is the plane going to crash?" they asked. "Close to New Year's," Doris answered. "Is it going to be us?" "No," Doris said, "but it's going to be real close."

At 7:30 P.M. on Friday, December 29, 1972, one of Eastern's new Tristar jets, the L-1011, landed in New York. It had come from Miami and would make a short layover before flying back. The entire cockpit crew—Captain Bob Loft, First Officer Bert Stockstill, and Second Officer Don Repo—had volunteered for Flight 401. The short round-trip flight would put

them home in Miami with their families for the holiday.

Captain Loft looked at his watch. A cabin crew was flying up from Miami to work the flight. But they were late, so a last-minute change was planned. The same cabin crew that had flown with the plane into New York would remain aboard. Among the crew was Doris Elliot.

Then, at 8:40 P.M., the scheduled cabin crew landed in New York. They rushed onto Flight 401. Doris Elliot and the others got off.

Flight 401 took off at 9:20 P.M., passengers and crew both in a holiday mood. By 11:30, Captain Loft had his landing instructions from Miami. Soon he gave the order to lower the landing gear. As the gear descended, a warning light flashed. Something seemed to be wrong with the nosewheel. Loft began to circle, and he set the automatic pilot, while the cockpit crew checked out the problem.

Within a minute the giant jet began to lose altitude. The automatic pilot had somehow disengaged. The crew was so busy looking into the problem indicated by the warning light for the nosewheel that no one noticed the altimeter dropping, and in the black of night there were no visual signs that the plane was descending. The flight recorder later revealed

Captain Loft's words as the earth suddenly loomed close in the light of the plane. "What's going on here?" he cried. The next instant Flight 401 crashed into the Everglades, killing 161 people, including the entire cockpit crew. Doris Elliot's vision had come true.

Four months after the disaster, in the spring of 1973, flight attendant Ginny Packard was working another Flight 401— also an L-1011—from New York to Miami. While she was in the galley preparing meals, a cloud about the size of a grapefruit appeared in front of her. Dumbfounded, she watched as the cloud formed a human face.

Ginny ran from the galley. Was she going crazy? She didn't think so. But who would believe she had just seen the ghost of Second Officer Don Repo?

A few weeks later, that same L-1011 was at Newark Airport in New Jersey, preparing to take off. When senior flight attendant Sis Patterson took a routine head count of passengers in the first-class section, she noticed an extra passenger—a man dressed in the uniform of an Eastern Airlines captain.

"Excuse me, Captain," she said, "I don't have you on my passenger list." The man stared straight ahead, as if he had not heard a word. "Sir," she repeated, "may I have your name?" Still no answer.

A second attendant approached the man and inquired if he was ill. He seemed to be in a daze. That attendant, too, got no response to her questions.

The two women called their captain for help. As he leaned over to talk to the man, his face registered shock and disbelief. "It's Bob Loft!" he announced. No one moved. There was total silence. Then the uniformed figure vanished. One moment he was there, the next he wasn't!

A number of other strange occurrences involving the crew of the ill-fated Flight 401 also took place on L-1011s. On at least five other occasions, either Captain Loft or Second Officer Repo materialized on the jets.

It was reported that Don Repo told one crew, "There will never be another crash of an L-1011. We will not let it happen." He is said to have warned another crew, "Watch out for fire on this airplane." Shortly thereafter, an engine caught fire. The crew was able to land the disabled plane safely.

Had ghosts actually appeared on those Eastern flights? The airline wasn't talking—for obvious reasons. Neither were most of the flight crews, who were afraid they would be fired if they spoke out. Then John Fuller entered the picture.

A well-respected science writer, Fuller, by his own admission, did not believe in ghosts. But he was a curious person. He was determined to get to the bottom of the mystery.

After months of coaxing the flight crews who had witnessed the incidents, he was able to get some people to tell their stories. Even then, they made him swear that he would never reveal their names. Fuller kept that promise.

The interviews convinced Fuller that he could not shrug off the incidents. Too many people, who had too much to lose to make up stories, claimed to have seen the ghosts. Still, Fuller wanted hard evidence of the ghosts' existence.

He tried mediums—people who claim to be able to contact the spirit world—but nothing they came up with convinced him. Then he decided to try using a Ouija board to reach the spirit of Don Repo. A Ouija board is a board on which are printed the letters of the alphabet, the numerals one to nine and zero, and the words *yes* and *no*. Users rest their fingertips lightly on a flat triangular marker and concentrate on the spirit they wish to contact. The marker will supposedly move around the board to the markings, spelling out messages from the spirit.

Using a Ouija board, Fuller got a lot of information about the plane crash. But none of it was the kind of hard evidence he demanded. Then he got two more messages—gibberish, or so he thought: *Did the mice leave that family closet?* and *To go into wastebasket pennies sit there boys room.* What could those messages mean? Fuller telephoned Repo's wife.

"Tell me," he said, "did you ever have mice in what you call your 'family

closet'?" Alice Repo was taken by surprise. "How did you know about that?" She explained that some mice had built a nest in the attic above their family room. The only way to get to the attic to set traps was through the family room closet.

Next Fuller asked, "Did Don have anything to do with some pennies in a wastebasket in your boy's room?" "This is amazing," Alice Repo said. "Don used to collect Indian head pennies. There's a small barrel full of them in our son's room."

John Fuller was satisfied. Only the Repos could have known those facts. As far as John Fuller was concerned, the ghosts of Flight 401 were indeed real. ■

Note: In accord with the wishes of the flight attendants, their real names have not been used.

*If you have been timed while reading this selection, enter your reading time below. Then turn to the Words per Minute table on page 154 and look up your reading speed (words per minute). Enter your reading speed on the graph on page 156.*

Turn to the Words per Minute table on page 154 and look up your reading speed (words per minute). Enter your reading speed on the graph on page 156.

| READING TIME: Unit 4 |
| --- |
| _____ : _____ |
| *Minutes*      *Seconds* |

# How well did you read?

- *Answer the four types of questions that follow. The directions for each type of question tell you how to mark your answers.*

- *When you have finished all four exercises, check your work by using the answer key on page 150. For each right answer, put a check mark (✔) on the line beside the box. For each wrong answer, write the correct answer on the line.*

- *For scoring each exercise, follow the directions below the questions.*

## A  FINDING THE MAIN IDEA

Look at the three statements below. One expresses the main idea of the story you just read. A good main idea statement answers two questions: it tells *who* or *what* is the subject of the story, and it answers the understood question *does what?* or *is what?* Another statement is *too broad*, it is vague and doesn't tell much about the topic of the story. The third statement is *too narrow*, it tells about only one part of the story.

Match the statements with the three answer choices below by writing the letter of each answer in the box in front of the statement it goes with.

**M—Main Idea      B—Too Broad      N—Too Narrow**

_____  ☐  1. Some people claim to have seen the ghosts of the crew of a jet that crashed.

_____  ☐  2. According to reports of reliable witnesses, ghosts of the crew of a downed Eastern Airlines L-1011 have appeared on a number of other L-1011 flights.

_____  ☐  3. The ghosts of Don Repo and Bob Loft warned several cabin crews of possible disasters.

_____  Score 15 points for a correct *M* answer

_____  Score 5 points for each correct *B* or *N* answer

_____  TOTAL SCORE: Finding the Main Idea

## B  RECALLING FACTS

How well do you remember the facts in the story you just read?
Put an *x* in the box in front of the correct answer to each of the
multiple choice questions below.

1. Flight 401 traveled regularly between
____ ☐ a. New York and Miami.
____ ☐ b. Miami and Washington.
____ ☐ c. Washington and New York.

2. The captain of the Flight 401 that crashed was
____ ☐ a. Bob Loft.
____ ☐ b. Bert Stockstill.
____ ☐ c. Don Repo.

3. Flight 401 crashed in
____ ☐ a. Florida.
____ ☐ b. Georgia.
____ ☐ c. New York.

4. John Fuller decided to investigate the reports of the
ghosts of Flight 401 because he
____ ☐ a. made his living as a ghost hunter.
____ ☐ b. was hired by Eastern to get to the bottom
          of things.
____ ☐ c. was curious to know the truth.

5. John Fuller persuaded witnesses to talk by
____ ☐ a. offering them money for their stories.
____ ☐ b. promising to keep their identities secret.
____ ☐ c. threatening to report them to their superiors.

Score 5 points for each correct answer

____ TOTAL SCORE: Recalling Facts

## C  MAKING INFERENCES

An inference is a judgment that is made or an idea that is
arrived at based on facts or on information that is given. You
make an inference when you understand something that is *not*
stated directly, but that is *implied*, or suggested by the facts that
are given.

Below are five statements that are judgments or ideas that
have been arrived at from the facts of the story. Write the letter
*C* in the box in front of each statement that is a correct inference. Write the letter *F* in front of each faulty inference.

**C—Correct Inference        F—Faulty Inference**

____ ☐ 1. L-101ls have a poor safety record.

____ ☐ 2. If the captain had been paying attention to the
           instruments, the plane would not have crashed.

____ ☐ 3. The ghosts of Flight 401 were trying to keep
           people from flying on L-101ls.

____ ☐ 4. As a result of John Fuller's investigation, Eastern
           Airlines stopped using L-101ls.

____ ☐ 5. Eastern Airlines felt that public reports of the
           ghosts would hurt the airline.

Score 5 points for each correct answer

____ TOTAL SCORE: Making Inferences

## D USING WORDS PRECISELY

Each of the numbered sentences below contains an underlined word or phrase from the story you have just read. Under the sentence are three definitions. One has the *same* meaning as the underlined word or phrase, one has *almost the same* meaning, and one has the *opposite* meaning. Match the definitions with the three answer choices by writing the letter that stands for each answer in the box in front of the definition it goes with.

**S—Same     A—Almost the Same     O—Opposite**

1. The left wing of the plane crumpled, and the jet <u>hurtled</u> into the swamp.

____ ☐ a. slipped

____ ☐ b. barreled

____ ☐ c. ran

2. They had faith in Doris's <u>premonitions</u>.

____ ☐ a. predictions

____ ☐ b. flashbacks

____ ☐ c. visions of the future

3. The flight recorder later revealed Captain Loft's words as the earth suddenly <u>loomed</u> close in the light of the plane.

____ ☐ a. vanished

____ ☐ b. appeared

____ ☐ c. arrived

4. As he leaned over to talk to the man, his face <u>registered</u> shock and disbelief.

____ ☐ a. recorded

____ ☐ b. hid

____ ☐ c. expressed

5. The crew was able to land the <u>disabled</u> plane safely.

____ ☐ a. crippled

____ ☐ b. weakened

____ ☐ c. undamaged

____ Score 3 points for each correct *S* answer
____ Score 1 point for each correct *A* or *O* answer

____ TOTAL SCORE: Using Words Precisely

● *Enter the four total scores in the spaces below, and add them together to find your Critical Reading Score. Then record your Critical Reading Score on the graph on page 157.*

____ Finding the Main Idea
____ Recalling Facts
____ Making Inferences
____ Using Words Precisely

____ CRITICAL READING SCORE: Unit 4

# Ocean-born Mary

In the town of Henniker, New Hampshire, stands a grand old house with a fascinating legend attached to it—a legend that some people would like to kill and others insist on preserving. For generations, stories have circulated of eerie happenings in and around the house. It has been said that lights would sometimes flicker on and off in an upstairs window, when no one was living in the house. The awful groans of a dying man have supposedly been heard in the woodyard behind the house. And now and then at dusk a coach drawn by four horses has reportedly taken shape at the front door. Inside the coach, a tall woman with flaming red hair sits, staring off into the distance. The woman, it is said, is the ghost of Ocean-born Mary, and this was once her house.

The story of Ocean-born Mary begins in Londonderry, Ireland, in 1720. A shipload of people were setting sail for a new life in the New World. They were bound for Londonderry, New Hampshire. Among those on board were James Wilson and his wife, Elizabeth, who was soon to bear their first child.

On July 28, as the voyage was drawing to a close, Elizabeth gave birth to her child. At about the same time, a lookout sighted land—America! Right after,

another lookout, perched high atop the mainmast, shouted, "Sail ho!"

At that cry, the captain's face remained calm, though he was anything but. He knew that his ship was easy prey for pirates, who were known to sail those waters. As he debated what to do, the strange ship drew nearer and fired a cannon. Then it broke out the skull and crossbones. Two boats were lowered over the side, and a group of fierce-looking men brandishing swords and pistols rowed swiftly to the immigrant ship and clambered onto its deck. At their head was a tall, dark-skinned man called Pedro. "Lash the men together!" he ordered. "Once we get the valuables, we'll kill them all!"

Pedro himself went below decks. He soon found what he was looking for: chests of silver, gold, and jewels. As he knelt to run his hands through the treasure, he heard a whimper. He drew his pistol and followed the sound—down the passageway to a locked cabin door. Pedro crashed through the door, pistol at the ready. What he faced was a terrified Elizabeth Wilson, lying in bed, her new-born baby cradled in her arms.

Pedro's fierce look disappeared. He lowered his pistol and approached. "Is it a girl?" he asked gently. "Yes," Elizabeth whispered. "Has she been named yet?" Pedro inquired. "No . . . not yet," came the hesitant reply.

Pedro leaned over to get a better look at the child. "My dear," he said to Elizabeth, "if you give this child my mother's name, I swear I will not harm this ship nor any of its passengers." A bewildered Elizabeth nodded yes. "Her name shall be Mary," Pedro said. Then he left the cabin.

Back on deck, he shouted a series of commands to his men. "Return the treasure! Release the men! We are leaving this vessel!" The pirates lowered themselves into their boats and pulled away to their own ship.

Shortly after, Pedro returned carrying a bundle. He went straight to Elizabeth's cabin. Thrusting the bundle at her, he said, "This is for little Mary's wedding dress." Pedro then left the ship and sailed away. Inside the package, Elizabeth found a bolt of pale green silk embroidered with flowers.

The immigrant ship landed safely in Boston. Shortly afterward, James Wilson died, and Elizabeth and her baby daughter went on to Londonderry, where a piece of land awaited them. The story of the tiny child who had saved a ship spread quickly. Everyone began calling her "Ocean-born Mary."

The years passed, and Mary grew to be a beautiful bright-eyed, red-haired woman, nearly six feet tall. A contemporary described her as being "elegant in her manners, resolute and determined, of strong mind, quick of comprehension, sharp in her conversation with a strong brogue and full of humor." When she married, she wore a wedding dress of green silk embroidered with flowers.

All to this point is true. The facts are of historical record. Here the legend begins.

Mary and her husband, James Wallace, lived in Londonderry and had four sons. When the boys were still very young, Mary's husband died. The pirate Pedro had long since retired from the sea, but he had never forgotten the child he had named for his mother. Hearing that Mary was widowed, Pedro decided to help. He went to Henniker, New Hampshire, accompanied by one of his ship's carpenters. Together they built a great house deep in the woods. Then Pedro sought out Mary.

Mary was happy to meet the pirate who had given her her name. She had long been curious about him. She found him to be both kindly and generous. "Care for me in my old age," Pedro said to Mary, "and I will see that you and your sons lack nothing." Mary agreed and went to live in Pedro's house. He gave her a coach-and-four to drive, and he made sure her children were well provided for.

Then one day Pedro left for the seacoast.

*The name Ocean-born Mary and the house pictured above have long been intertwined in a romantic legend featuring pirates, buried treasure, murder, and ghosts. Historians claim that the story is bunk. But Ocean-born Mary, whose gravestone is pictured on the right, was a real person. Just what is the truth in this story?*

43

When he returned, he was accompanied by a pirate. The two carried a huge chest, which they lugged deep into the woods and buried. When the last shovelful of earth had been thrown, a cry was heard in the night. Pedro returned from the woods alone. His companion was never seen again.

Months later, Mary returned from a drive in her coach-and-four to find the house empty. Where was Pedro? She found him behind the house, dead, his heart pierced by a cutlass. Pedro's body was buried under the huge hearthstone in the kitchen of the great house, where he had often said he wished to be placed.

The years went by, and one by one, Mary's sons married and left home. Mary stayed on alone in the house Pedro had built for her. She died there in 1814, at the age of eighty-four. Mary's ghost regularly visited the house, usually around sunset.

In recent years, the legend has distressed the people who live in the house. There is no ghost, they claim. And they wish people would stop bothering them.

First of all, the house, which has come to be called the Ocean-born Mary House, was not Mary's at all. It was built by her son Robert. Mary never lived there.

Historical records show that Mary did have four sons, but she also had a daughter. And Mary's husband did not die until he was eighty-one years old. Mary was seventy-one at the time—hardly the beautiful young widow of the legend. If Pedro had still been alive at that time, he would have been about a hundred. He never bought any land in Henniker or went looking for Mary Wallace.

In 1798, when she was seventy-eight years old, Mary left Londonderry to live with her son William in Henniker—about a mile from Robert's house. She lived there until her death. Mary was buried in the cemetery behind the Henniker Town Hall. A slate headstone marks her grave. On it are inscribed the words "In Memory of Widow Mary Wallace who died Feb. 13, 1814 in the 94th year of her age."

How did such a wild legend grow up around her name? It was all part of a money-making scheme. In 1917 a man named Louis Roy bought the Robert Wallace house, which had long been vacant and was in bad condition. He moved in with his mother and renovated the house, filling it with valuable antiques. Then he started the story about Mary and Pedro, the ghost, the buried treasure, and the cries in the woodyard. His story grew and grew, and many people began to believe it. Newspapers and magazines spread the story. People began to come from all over. Mr. Roy gave tours of the house for an admission fee. He even rented shovels for fifty cents apiece, so that folks could dig for the buried treasure.

Mr. Roy died in 1965, but by that time the legend had taken on a life of its own. The family that bought the house is still plagued by people wanting to see the ghost. Although the story has been proved to be a fake, some folks just refuse to believe the facts. It seems they'd rather cling to the more colorful fiction. A good ghost story dies hard. What would Mary and Pedro say if they knew? ■

*If you have been timed while reading this selection, enter your reading time below. Then turn to the Words per Minute table on page 154 and look up your reading speed (words per minute). Enter your reading speed on the graph on page 156.*

READING TIME: Unit 5

_____ : _____
*Minutes*     *Seconds*

# How well did you read?

- *Answer the four types of questions that follow. The directions for each type of question tell you how to mark your answers.*

- *When you have finished all four exercises, check your work by using the answer key on page 150. For each right answer, put a check mark (✓) on the line beside the box. For each wrong answer, write the correct answer on the line.*

- *For scoring each exercise, follow the directions below the questions.*

## A FINDING THE MAIN IDEA

Look at the three statements below. One expresses the main idea of the story you just read. A good main idea statement answers two questions: it tells *who* or *what* is the subject of the story, and it answers the understood question *does what?* or *is what?* Another statement is *too broad*, it is vague and doesn't tell much about the topic of the story. The third statement is *too narrow*, it tells about only one part of the story.

Match the statements with the three answer choices below by writing the letter of each answer in the box in front of the statement it goes with.

**M—Main Idea    B—Too Broad    N—Too Narrow**

_____ ☐ 1. The story of Ocean-born Mary has captured people's imaginations for generations.

_____ ☐ 2. Ocean-born Mary was born at sea and named by a pirate.

_____ ☐ 3. Ocean-born Mary was a real historical figure around whom a fantastic legend was woven.

_____ Score 15 points for a correct *M* answer

_____ Score 5 points for each correct *B* or *N* answer

_____ TOTAL SCORE: Finding the Main Idea

## B RECALLING FACTS

How well do you remember the facts in the story you just read?
Put an *x* in the box in front of the correct answer to each of the
multiple choice questions below.

1. The story of Ocean-born Mary takes place mainly
   - ___ ☐ a. in Ireland.
   - ___ ☐ b. in New Hampshire.
   - ___ ☐ c. on board a ship.

2. Mary Wallace lived most of her life in
   - ___ ☐ a. Boston, Massachusetts.
   - ___ ☐ b. Londonderry, New Hampshire.
   - ___ ☐ c. Henniker, New Hampshire.

3. Pedro gave Elizabeth a bundle that contained
   - ___ ☐ a. a bolt of cloth.
   - ___ ☐ b. the treasure his men had collected.
   - ___ ☐ c. his mother's wedding gown.

4. A few years after her husband's death, Ocean-born
   Mary went to live with
   - ___ ☐ a. her son William.
   - ___ ☐ b. her son Robert.
   - ___ ☐ c. Louis Roy.

5. Ocean-born Mary had
   - ___ ☐ a. two sons.
   - ___ ☐ b. four sons.
   - ___ ☐ c. four sons and a daughter.

Score 5 points for each correct answer

___ TOTAL SCORE: Recalling Facts

## C MAKING INFERENCES

An inference is a judgment that is made or an idea that is
arrived at based on facts or on information that is given. You
make an inference when you understand something that is *not*
stated directly, but that is *implied*, or suggested by the facts that
are given.

Below are five statements that are judgments or ideas that
have been arrived at from the facts of the story. Write the letter
*C* in the box in front of each statement that is a correct inference. Write the letter *F* in front of each faulty inference.

**C—Correct Inference          F—Faulty Inference**

- ___ ☐ 1. After Pedro spared the ship on which Mary
  Wallace was born, he gave up pirating.

- ___ ☐ 2. Mary Wallace did hope that someday she would
  get to meet Captain Pedro.

- ___ ☐ 3. Pedro loved his mother.

- ___ ☐ 4. Mary Wallace led an ordinary life.

- ___ ☐ 5. Mary's son Robert did not want his mother in
  his house.

Score 5 points for each correct answer

___ TOTAL SCORE: Making Inferences

## D USING WORDS PRECISELY

Each of the numbered sentences below contains an underlined word or phrase from the story you have just read. Under the sentence are three definitions. One has the *same* meaning as the underlined word or phrase, one has *almost the same* meaning, and one has the *opposite* meaning. Match the definitions with the three answer choices by writing the letter that stands for each answer in the box in front of the definition it goes with.

**S—Same     A—Almost the Same     O—Opposite**

1. Two boats were lowered over the side, and a group of fierce-looking men <u>brandishing</u> swords and pistols rowed swiftly to the immigrant ship.

   ____ ☐ a. waving

   ____ ☐ b. carrying

   ____ ☐ c. holding still

2. "No . . . not yet," came the <u>hesitant</u> reply.

   ____ ☐ a. fearful

   ____ ☐ b. firm

   ____ ☐ c. faltering

3. "Care for me in my old age," Pedro said to Mary, "and I will see that you and your sons <u>lack</u> nothing."

   ____ ☐ a. have

   ____ ☐ b. require

   ____ ☐ c. do without

4. In recent years, the legend has <u>distressed</u> the people who live in the house.

   ____ ☐ a. upset

   ____ ☐ b. pleased

   ____ ☐ c. outraged

5. The family that bought the house was <u>plagued</u> by people wanting to see the ghost.

   ____ ☐ a. irritated

   ____ ☐ b. tormented

   ____ ☐ c. soothed

____ Score 3 points for each correct *S* answer

____ Score 1 point for each correct *A* or *O* answer

____ TOTAL SCORE: Using Words Precisely

● *Enter the four total scores in the spaces below, and add them together to find your Critical Reading Score. Then record your Critical Reading Score on the graph on page 157.*

_____ Finding the Main Idea

_____ Recalling Facts

_____ Making Inferences

_____ Using Words Precisely

_____ CRITICAL READING SCORE: Unit 5

# The Case of the Missing Secretary

In the early 1900s, when Hester Holt arrived in Denver, Colorado, Denver was still very much a small town. That fact appealed to Hester, who was very much a small-town girl. She wanted to improve her life, and she was sure that Denver was the place to do it. She found a room in a house run by a Mrs. Britton. With her typing skills, Hester had no trouble finding a job as a secretary.

From Hester's first day on the job, Mrs. Bell, her employer, was more than satisfied with Hester's work. Hester did everything that was asked of her and more. And when she was sick, which was seldom, she was sure to notify Mrs. Bell. That was why her failure to show up one day without sending word was so strange.

Concerned, Mrs. Bell questioned Hester's coworker Stella Dean. "Hester didn't seem sick yesterday, did she, Stella?" "No, she was very cheerful, in fact," Stella replied. "I'm sure she'll be here tomorrow."

When Hester did not show up for work the following day, Mrs. Bell decided to send Stella to investigate. "Go check her rooming house to see what you can discover," Mrs. Bell ordered. "Perhaps something has happened to her."

Stella returned with unsettling news. "Her landlady says that Hester has gone away without telling anyone," reported Stella, bursting into tears.

Mrs. Bell found it difficult to believe that Hester would do such a thing. But when she herself talked to Mrs. Britton, it was just as Stella had said. After leaving the office the previous day, Hester had not returned to her room. It was as if she had vanished into thin air.

Mrs. Britton did have the address of Hester's sister, which she gave to Mrs. Bell. "Whenever Hester went away, she asked me to forward her mail there," the landlady explained.

Hester's sister, however, could shed no light on the matter. She had not heard from Hester in over a month. "But if anyone knows where she is, it's Pete Simpkins," she said.

Pete Simpkins, Hester's fiancé, was as mystified by Hester's disappearance as Hester's sister was. "I haven't seen her since the day she left you," Simpkins told Mrs. Bell. He had been in the country that day, he said, supervising the building of a farm. Cycling home, he had seen Hester Holt and Stella Dean riding in a buggy.

"Are you sure?" asked Mrs. Bell. "I'll swear to it," said Simpkins. "I did think it was strange, though, since I know that Hester and Stella don't get along." He explained that he had once been engaged to Stella, then had broken it off because of Stella's uncontrollable temper. "Stella was furious when Hester and I started seeing each other," said Simpkins.

The next day Mrs. Bell questioned Stella Dean. "Did you go for a drive with Hester the night she disappeared?" she asked. "The last time I saw Hester was when she left the office," said Stella. Although she did admit that she and Simpkins had once been engaged, Stella denied that she had any animosity toward Hester. "We were always on the best of terms," she insisted.

When Hester was still missing the next day, Mrs. Bell called the police. "It's all very mysterious," she told them. "Please do what you can to find her."

The police investigation revealed that Simpkins had been telling the truth. Another witness had seen the two girls riding out of town in a buggy on the day Hester disappeared. Hester had rented the buggy from a car dealer, who confirmed that she had driven off in it alone. The buggy was returned that evening, when the dealer's wife was on duty. She took payment from a woman, but she could not describe her. It had been dark, and the woman had been bundled against the cold.

Where was Stella Dean that evening? Her mother claimed that Stella had come

*When Hester Holt disappeared without a trace, her friends began to worry. Where could she have gone? The look of fear in the eyes of one young woman said that she knew more than she was telling. And when typewriters started typing and briefcases started moving on their own, people knew for sure that something strange was afoot.*

home from the office and stayed home all night.

Another witness confused the issue by stating that she had seen Hester Holt entering Mrs. Britton's rooming house on the night in question.

Although they suspected foul play, the police were forced to drop the case for lack of evidence. Mrs. Bell gave up hoping that Hester would return and hired a replacement, whose name was Vera Cummings.

On her first day in the office, Vera sat in Hester Holt's chair, next to Stella Dean. She soon began to shiver. "Why is it that I start shivering whenever I sit next to you, Stella?" Vera asked. "It must be your imagination," replied Stella.

But Vera was so uncomfortable that she moved several feet away. Some time later she remarked, "My, Stella, you certainly have long legs!" "What on earth do you mean?" demanded Stella. "Your feet keep kicking mine under the table." "You're imagining things again," Stella snapped. But Vera couldn't help noticing that Stella turned very pale.

Three days later, when Vera and Stella were taking a break, Vera asked, "Stella, who is that tall, good-looking woman I've seen following you into the building? I've watched her stand behind you in the elevator, but then she disappears. Does she

work in another office?" A frightened look came over Stella's face, but she denied having seen the woman Vera described. "You were dreaming," she said.

Mrs. Bell had overheard the conversation, and her interest was aroused. "Can you describe the woman, Vera?" she asked. Mrs. Bell's eyes grew wide as Vera gave a detailed description of a woman who sounded exactly like Hester Holt.

The next morning the three women arrived at the office at the same time. As they stood outside the door, they heard the sound of typing. "Maybe Hester has come back!" said Mrs. Bell hopefully. Stella remained quiet, but she looked strangely frightened.

When they entered the room, the three women stopped in their tracks. The typewriter was indeed typing away, but there was no one there. The room was completely empty!

Complaining of a headache, Stella left work early. She stayed out for several weeks. When she finally returned to the office, Pete Simpkins met her at the door, a huge smile on his face. "She never told me, but she's back!" he exclaimed. "What are you talking about, Pete?" asked Stella crossly.

"I'm talking about Hester," Pete answered excitedly. "I just saw her walk into the building." Without saying a word, Stella whirled and ran through the door. Vera Cummings, who had also been about to enter the building, had watched Stella's reaction with interest. "Pete," she asked, "are you sure it was Hester you saw?" "Absolutely," Pete insisted. Then he described the woman he had seen. "Why, that sounds just like the woman I've seen following Stella!" Vera exclaimed. "This is all very strange."

The day after Stella's return, things got even stranger. Since Mrs. Bell was out sick, Vera and Stella were alone in the office. At one point Vera glanced at Stella and saw that she had a horrified look on her face. She was staring at a briefcase, which was rocking back and forth for no apparent reason. On the briefcase were the initials H. H.

Later the two women were leaving for lunch when Vera, startled by a sharp cry, turned to see Stella staring into a mirror. Stella's own reflection stared back at her. But behind her shoulder was another face, pale and with dark, piercing eyes. It was the face of the woman Vera had seen following Stella—the face, Vera was sure, of Hester Holt.

Stella ran from the room, the door slamming behind her. When Vera tried to follow, the door would not open, though she used all her strength. Perplexed, Vera was trying to decide what to do when the door suddenly swung open by itself. On the other side of the door, Stella Dean lay sprawled on the floor.

The police report listed the cause of death as accidental. According to Stella's mother, her daughter had suffered from a bad heart. Only Vera knew that Stella had died of fright.

Stella Dean was known for her bad temper. Had it finally gotten the best of her? Had she murdered her rival, Hester Holt, in a fit of jealous rage, and then buried the body by the side of the road on the night Pete Simpkins had seen the two women in the buggy? If so, had the ghost of Hester Holt gotten her revenge? The police report had no answers.

Nor did the strange story end with Stella's death. When Vera Cummings returned to work, she saw two women entering the office. One was Stella Dean, who looked just as she had in life, except that she was obviously in terror. The other woman followed close behind her. There was no mistaking the tall, slender figure of Hester Holt. ■

*If you have been timed while reading this selection, enter your reading time below. Then turn to the Words per Minute table on page 154 and look up your reading speed (words per minute). Enter your reading speed on the graph on page 156.*

READING TIME: Unit 6

_____ : _____
*Minutes*           *Seconds*

# How well did you read?

- *Answer the four types of questions that follow. The directions for each type of question tell you how to mark your answers.*

- *When you have finished all four exercises, check your work by using the answer key on page 150. For each right answer, put a check mark (✓) on the line beside the box. For each wrong answer, write the correct answer on the line.*

- *For scoring each exercise, follow the directions below the questions.*

## A  FINDING THE MAIN IDEA

Look at the three statements below. One expresses the main idea of the story you just read. A good main idea statement answers two questions: it tells *who* or *what* is the subject of the story, and it answers the understood question *does what?* or *is what?* Another statement is *too broad,* it is vague and doesn't tell much about the topic of the story. The third statement is *too narrow,* it tells about only one part of the story.

Match the statements with the three answer choices below by writing the letter of each answer in the box in front of the statement it goes with.

**M—Main Idea      B—Too Broad      N—Too Narrow**

____  ☐  1. A secretary who had mysteriously disappeared haunted the place in which she had worked, frightening her coworker and possible murderer to death.

____  ☐  2. Stella Dean was suspected of murdering her coworker, Hester Holt, in a fit of jealousy.

____  ☐  3. The mysterious disappearance of a young woman and the sudden, unexplained death of her coworker in the early 1900s left those close to the events wondering if ghosts and foul play were involved.

____  Score 15 points for a correct *M* answer

____  Score 5 points for each correct *B* or *N* answer

____  TOTAL SCORE: Finding the Main Idea

## B ■ RECALLING FACTS

How well do you remember the facts in the story you just read?
Put an *x* in the box in front of the correct answer to each of the
multiple choice questions below.

1. This story took place in
____ ☐ a. Sacramento, California.
____ ☐ b. Denver, Colorado.
____ ☐ c. Portland, Oregon.

2. Mrs. Bell was Hester Holt's
____ ☐ a. landlady.
____ ☐ b. boss.
____ ☐ c. sister.

3. On the day Hester disappeared, Pete Simpkins saw her
____ ☐ a. leaving the office with Stella Dean.
____ ☐ b. entering the rooming house where she lived.
____ ☐ c. riding in a buggy with Stella Dean.

4. Stella was angry with Hester because
____ ☐ a. their employer favored Hester.
____ ☐ b. Hester was engaged to marry Stella's former
fiancé.
____ ☐ c. Hester made more money than she did.

5. The police
____ ☐ a. could not solve the case.
____ ☐ b. found that Stella had murdered Hester.
____ ☐ c. suspected that Hester had merely left town.

Score 5 points for each correct answer

____ TOTAL SCORE: Recalling Facts

## C ■ MAKING INFERENCES

An inference is a judgment that is made or an idea that is
arrived at based on facts or on information that is given. You
make an inference when you understand something that is *not*
stated directly, but that is *implied*, or suggested by the facts that
are given.

Below are five statements that are judgments or ideas that
have been arrived at from the facts of the story. Write the letter
*C* in the box in front of each statement that is a correct inference. Write the letter *F* in front of each faulty inference.

**C—Correct Inference    F—Faulty Inference**

____ ☐ 1. Hester Holt was a very responsible person.

____ ☐ 2. The police did not suspect Stella Dean of having
any part in Hester's disappearance.

____ ☐ 3. Stella Dean lived with her mother.

____ ☐ 4. Hester and her sister did not get along very well.

____ ☐ 5. Vera Cummings believed that Stella had murdered
Hester.

Score 5 points for each correct answer

____ TOTAL SCORE: Making Inferences

## D USING WORDS PRECISELY

Each of the numbered sentences below contains an underlined word or phrase from the story you have just read. Under the sentence are three definitions. One has the *same* meaning as the underlined word or phrase, one has *almost the same* meaning, and one has the *opposite* meaning. Match the definitions with the three answer choices by writing the letter that stands for each answer in the box in front of the definition it goes with.

**S—Same    A—Almost the Same    O—Opposite**

1. Stella returned with underlined unsettling news.

____ ☐ a. calming

____ ☐ b. disturbing

____ ☐ c. frightening

2. Pete Simpkins, Hester's fiancé, was as mystified by Hester's disappearance as Hester's sister was.

____ ☐ a. puzzled

____ ☐ b. certain

____ ☐ c. confused

3. Although she did admit that she and Simpkins had once been engaged, Stella denied that she had any animosity toward Hester.

____ ☐ a. goodwill

____ ☐ b. dislike

____ ☐ c. hostility

4. Mrs. Bell had overheard the conversation, and her interest was aroused.

____ ☐ a. increased

____ ☐ b. stirred

____ ☐ c. deadened

5. Perplexed, Vera was trying to decide what to do when the door suddenly swung open by itself.

____ ☐ a. muddled

____ ☐ b. puzzled

____ ☐ c. with a clear mind

____ Score 3 points for each correct S answer

____ Score 1 point for each correct A or O answer

____ TOTAL SCORE: Using Words Precisely

● *Enter the four total scores in the spaces below, and add them together to find your Critical Reading Score. Then record your Critical Reading Score on the graph on page 157.*

_____ Finding the Main Idea
_____ Recalling Facts
_____ Making Inferences
_____ Using Words Precisely
_____ CRITICAL READING SCORE: Unit 6

To the edge of the rugged cliff that dropped to the sea, the ghost stallion bore Matthew Lee, forcing him to gaze upon the grisly scene from his past. From that time forward, Matthew Lee was a changed man, living in terror of the fate he feared lay in store for him. He knew there was no escape.

54

# The Ghost Ship of Matthew Lee

Centuries ago, a small boy named Matthew Lee dreamed of commanding his own sailing ship. When he grew up, that dream came true. Matthew loved standing watch at the wheel, feeling his ship plowing through the waves. He loved the touch of salt spray, the fresh sea air. But one thing he did not love. That was the poor living he made. Above all, Matthew Lee longed to be rich.

Exactly when the opportunity arose is not known, but one day Matthew Lee saw a chance to change his situation. While taking on cargo in a Spanish port, he was approached by a beautiful woman. "Captain Lee," she said, "I am told your vessel is available for charter. Is that true?" "I would be willing to take you anywhere, Señora," said Lee with a smile.

At that the woman explained that she was recently widowed. Her husband had died fighting for Spain. She wanted to leave sad memories behind and return to her native land, America.

Lee was intrigued. The woman clearly had money. Accompanying her were several servants bearing chests that held a fortune in jewels.

One problem arose, however. The woman insisted that her favorite horse, a spirited white stallion, be allowed to travel with her. Lee balked at the idea of carrying such a large animal on a long ocean voyage. But he finally agreed to have a stall built below decks for the horse.

Was it then that Lee decided on his evil plan? Or did he change from sea captain to pirate sometime later, during the long Atlantic crossing? We will never know. But it was not until his ship entered Block Island Sound that Lee put his plan into action.

Somewhere along the way, he had conspired with his crew. As they reached a point midway between Point Judith, on the southern tip of Rhode Island, and Block Island, eight miles off the coast, Lee gave a signal. The crew immediately moved into action. As the passengers slept, the men quietly stabbed them all, one by one, to death. All, that is, except the señora. Lee had other plans for her.

He bounded below and broke into her cabin. Standing over her, he demanded, "Señora, become my slave and your life is spared." Though terrified, the woman leaped for the door and dashed up onto the deck. Lee, cutlass at his side, merely laughed. Where could she go? There was no escape.

On deck, Lee approached the trembling woman and once again offered his bargain: "Be mine and you may live!" In answer the woman climbed onto the ship's rail and threw herself into the sea. Lee rushed to the rail just in time to see her head disappear beneath the waves. Enraged, he ordered her stallion thrown overboard. The huge animal fought wildly for its life, but in the end it joined its mistress.

Lee and his men gleefully set about divvying up the woman's riches. Perhaps the sight of so much wealth proved more than the poor sailors could deal with, for they fell to fighting among themselves. In the fracas, the ship was set afire. Lee and his friends in the crew escaped with their loot in a small boat. They rowed the mile or so to Block Island, hauled their boat onto the sands, and watched as the ship, now brightly ablaze, drifted north. Lee was pleased. He trusted that the sea would swallow any evidence of his crime.

The Block Islanders asked no questions of the free-spending newcomers. All went well for nearly a year. Then, on the anniversary of their crime, Lee and his men held a celebration. Their thirsts quenched with rum, the pirates reveled well into the night. At some point they noticed a faint glow upon the sea, off the north coast of the island. At first the glow appeared no brighter than a star. But it gradually drew nearer and increased in brightness, and as it did it revealed itself to be a flaming ship. It was the very ship the murderers had set afire one year earlier!

As Lee and his men watched in horror, in the glow of the fire a white stallion, its mane streaming water, rose from the sea and cantered up to the pirates. It fixed its fiery eyes on Matthew Lee. Unable to stop himself, Lee climbed onto the stallion, which then galloped to a cliff overlooking the blazing ship. Lee was forced to look down upon the bodies of the people he and his crew had murdered.

The apparition slowly faded with the coming of dawn, and Lee was allowed to return home. But he could no longer live in peace. The islanders too had seen the burning ship, and they recognized Lee for the villain he was. They now shunned him. Even his own men turned their backs on him, for they feared they would share in his doom.

The experience changed Lee profoundly. Overnight, he became an old man. Day after day, alone and frightened, he wandered the shores of the island. He guessed what lay in store for him if he stayed there, but he could not escape. The only way to the mainland was by sea, and Matthew Lee was too frightened to take that route.

Another year passed. On the second anniversary of the massacre, Lee's worst fears were realized. Once again the burning ship appeared and the great white stallion rose from the sea. And once again Lee was powerless to keep himself from riding the beast. This time, however, rather than carrying Lee to the cliff, the stallion galloped to the beach, plunged into the sea, and headed straight for the burning ship.

Matthew Lee and the great white stallion were never seen again. The horse had fulfilled its mission. It had avenged the death of its mistress.

The story does not end there, however. There are Block Islanders who swear that once a year an eerie glow appears on the waters off the island's north shore. Is it just a quirk of the weather, as outsiders claim? Or could it be the ghost of Matthew Lee's ship, reminding people of the terrible crime that was committed in those waters? ∎

*If you have been timed while reading this selection, enter your reading time below. Then turn to the Words per Minute table on page 154 and look up your reading speed (words per minute). Enter your reading speed on the graph on page 156.*

READING TIME: Unit 7

_____ : _____
*Minutes*     *Seconds*

# How well did you read?

- *Answer the four types of questions that follow. The directions for each type of question tell you how to mark your answers.*

- *When you have finished all four exercises, check your work by using the answer key on page 150. For each right answer, put a check mark (✔) on the line beside the box. For each wrong answer, write the correct answer on the line.*

- *For scoring each exercise, follow the directions below the questions.*

## A FINDING THE MAIN IDEA

Look at the three statements below. One expresses the main idea of the story you just read. A good main idea statement answers two questions: it tells *who* or *what* is the subject of the story, and it answers the understood question *does what?* or *is what?* Another statement is *too broad,* it is vague and doesn't tell much about the topic of the story. The third statement is *too narrow,* it tells about only one part of the story.

Match the statements with the three answer choices below by writing the letter of each answer in the box in front of the statement it goes with.

**M—Main Idea      B—Too Broad      N—Too Narrow**

_____ ☐ 1. It is said that each year a strange light that some people believe is Lee's burning ship appears in the waters off Block Island.

_____ ☐ 2. Matthew Lee lived a life of crime and was eventually punished by ghosts for his evil deeds.

_____ ☐ 3. For murdering people at sea, Matthew Lee was punished by being taken to an apparition of the burning ship by a ghostly stallion.

_____ Score 15 points for a correct *M* answer

_____ Score 5 points for each correct *B* or *N* answer

_____ TOTAL SCORE: Finding the Main Idea

## B  RECALLING FACTS

How well do you remember the facts in the story you just read?
Put an x in the box in front of the correct answer to each of the
multiple choice questions below.

1. Matthew Lee took the señora aboard ship in
____  ☐ a. England
____  ☐ b. Spain.
____  ☐ c. Italy.

2. Block Island is off the coast of
____  ☐ a. Rhode Island.
____  ☐ b. South Carolina.
____  ☐ c. Maine.

3. After the señora leaped into the sea, Captain Lee
____  ☐ a. tried to save her.
____  ☐ b. ordered his men to set fire to the ship.
____  ☐ c. ordered the stallion pushed into the sea.

4. The main reason Captain Lee was interested in taking
the woman aboard his ship was that
____  ☐ a. she was beautiful.
____  ☐ b. she had a lot of money.
____  ☐ c. he wanted to help her.

5. Lee was taken to his final punishment
____  ☐ a. two years after his crime.
____  ☐ b. one year after his crime.
____  ☐ c. three years after his crime.

Score 5 points for each correct answer

____  TOTAL SCORE: Recalling Facts

## C  MAKING INFERENCES

An inference is a judgment that is made or an idea that is
arrived at based on facts or on information that is given. You
make an inference when you understand something that is *not*
stated directly, but that is *implied,* or suggested by the facts that
are given.

Below are five statements that are judgments or ideas that
have been arrived at from the facts of the story. Write the letter
*C* in the box in front of each statement that is a correct inference. Write the letter *F* in front of each faulty inference.

**C—Correct Inference     F—Faulty Inference**

____  ☐ 1. After seeing the ghost ship for the first time,
Matthew Lee became filled with sorrow for the
crime he had committed.

____  ☐ 2. The Block Islanders didn't care if Lee and his
men were murderers.

____  ☐ 3. The captains of sailing ships in Matthew Lee's
day did not earn very much money.

____  ☐ 4. The woman jumped overboard because she
thought she had a chance of swimming to shore.

____  ☐ 5. The ghostly stallion did not return to punish the
members of Matthew Lee's crew.

Score 5 points for each correct answer

____  TOTAL SCORE: Making Inferences

# D USING WORDS PRECISELY

Each of the numbered sentences below contains an underlined word or phrase from the story you have just read. Under the sentence are three definitions. One has the *same* meaning as the underlined word or phrase, one has *almost the same* meaning, and one has the *opposite* meaning. Match the definitions with the three answer choices by writing the letter that stands for each answer in the box in front of the definition it goes with.

**S—Same    A—Almost the Same    O—Opposite**

1. Lee balked at the idea of carrying such a large animal on a long ocean voyage.

____ ☐ a. resisted

____ ☐ b. questioned

____ ☐ c. accepted

2. He bounded below and broke into her cabin.

____ ☐ a. leaped

____ ☐ b. crept

____ ☐ c. charged

3. In the fracas, the ship was set afire.

____ ☐ a. brawl

____ ☐ b. efforts to come to peace

____ ☐ c. quarrel

4. Lee and his men gleefully set about divvying up the woman's riches.

____ ☐ a. uniting

____ ☐ b. dividing

____ ☐ c. sharing

5. Their thirsts quenched with rum, the pirates reveled well into the night.

____ ☐ a. rested

____ ☐ b. played

____ ☐ c. partied

____ Score 3 points for each correct S answer
____ Score 1 point for each correct A or O answer

____ TOTAL SCORE: Using Words Precisely

● *Enter the four total scores in the spaces below, and add them together to find your Critical Reading Score. Then record your Critical Reading Score on the graph on page 157.*

_____ Finding the Main Idea
_____ Recalling Facts
_____ Making Inferences
_____ Using Words Precisely

_____ CRITICAL READING SCORE: Unit 7

# GROUP TWO

It is said that moonlit nights sometimes set the stage for an eerie phenomenon at the Castillo de San Marcos in St. Augustine, Florida. The event involves the great Seminole chief Osceola—well, part of him, anyway. His head. What does Osceola have to do with the fort? Why does his head seem to be lingering? Those questions are best answered in the story of the life and death of this strong, proud man who led his people in the struggle to keep their homeland.

# Osceola's Head

It had been another busy day at Castillo de San Marcos. Hundreds of tourists had visited the old fort in St. Augustine, Florida. They had peered into the musty dungeons. They had taken pictures of one another on the wide battlements. As the day came to a close, they solemnly watched the flag being lowered.

A few people lingered long after the sun had set. They glanced expectantly, and perhaps nervously, at the high walls of the fort, bathed in silvery moonlight. Would they see it? they wondered. Would they see the ghostly head of Osceola floating above the fort?

To understand what those people were looking for, we must go back in time to a warm October day in 1837. On that day a tall Indian man stood with his hands clasped behind his back, gazing intently into the waters of a shallow creek. He was Osceola, a proud chief of the Seminole tribe of Florida.

Osceola's reflection revealed a handsome man with dark eyes, high cheekbones, and a light complexion. He owed the color of his skin to his father, an English trader. But he was very much an Indian, for his mother was a Creek. The Seminole were originally part of the Creek confederation of tribes in Alabama and Georgia. When some of them moved south into Florida,

they became known as Seminole, meaning "runaways."

Osceola was not admiring his reflection in the water that day. He was deep in thought. It was the day the Seminole might finally get their lands back.

For more than a hundred years, the Seminole had lived peacefully in Florida. Then white settlers had taken their lands. In 1835 the federal government attempted to force the Seminole to sign a treaty that would require them to move west to what is now Oklahoma.

"Why should we leave our homelands?" Osceola asked. Most of the other Seminole leaders agreed with him. They voted not to sign the treaty. Instead, they vowed to fight for their rights until the last drop of Seminole blood had been shed. Osceola was chosen to lead the struggle.

The fighting began, and it was terrible. The Seminole raided village after village, killing the settlers. In turn, government soldiers chased the Seminole back into the swampy forests of Florida. Many lives were lost on both sides, but it was clear that the Seminole were not about to surrender. Finally, General Thomas Jesup, the leader of the government forces, had an idea. He invited Osceola to meet with him under a flag of truce to talk peace.

Osceola agreed to talk, for he too was

tired of the bloodshed. His body ached with weariness brought on by bouts of yellow fever that sapped his strength. He was eager to end the war.

The day of the meeting arrived. Osceola, together with a handful of other Seminole leaders whom he had brought with him, waited at the appointed place. Each warrior had a square of white cloth—the flag of truce—tied to his rifle.

There was to be no peace talk, however. General Jesup had laid a trap, not the groundwork for peace. Two hundred soldiers rode up and seized Osceola and his companions.

The Seminole leaders were thrown into jail in the old fort of Castillo de San Marcos in St. Augustine. When word of General Jesup's deception got out, the whole country was outraged. Still, Jesup refused to release Osceola. He believed that without Osceola's leadership the Seminole resistance would collapse. It did not, and the war went on.

As 1837 drew to a close, Osceola, who had been joined by his family, was moved to a prison in Fort Moultrie, South Carolina. The fever that had long plagued him now confined him to his bed. He knew his end was near.

On the morning of January 30, 1838, Osceola readied himself for death. He dressed in his finest clothes. Around his head he wound a turban. In it he stuck three feathers: one red, one white, and one blue. He painted half of his face and neck with red war paint. Without a word, he solemnly shook the hands of his family and friends. Then he called for his favorite scalping knife. Clasping the knife, he crossed his hands on his chest. He drew one more breath, smiled, and died. Osceola was about thirty-five years old.

Dr. Frederick Wheedon, who had been treating Osceola at the prison, prepared the chief's body for burial. The funeral that followed drew hundreds of admirers who wanted to pay their respects to the great warrior and leader. How surprised they would have been to learn what was—or rather what was not—in the wooden coffin they saw lowered into the ground.

Did Osceola's death mean the end of war with the Seminole? No, indeed. In fact, the fighting continued for five more years. Finally, realizing they would never defeat the Seminole, the government simply quit fighting. To this day, the Seminole own their lands in Florida. They are the only Indian tribe ever to refuse to sign a treaty with the government.

Osceola was eventually returned to his home. Many years after his death, when Florida had become the twenty-seventh state, the government decided that Osceola should be reburied in the land he had fought so hard to defend.

When his coffin was dug up for the move, officials decided to open it and look inside. What a surprise they got! Osceola's skull was missing. It seems that Dr. Wheedon, for reasons he never disclosed, had cut off Osceola's head when he prepared the body for burial. He took the head to his home in St. Augustine. It passed through many hands over the years, finally ending up in a museum in New York City. In 1866 a fire ravaged part of the museum, and Osceola's head was destroyed.

Or was it? Many visitors to the old fort of Castillo de San Marcos claim to have seen the head. It is said that on moonlit nights the head often appears, hovering above the very cell in which Osceola was imprisoned. It is wrapped in a turban decorated with three feathers: one red, one white, and one blue.

Is it possible that Osceola's ghostly head does appear over the fort, or do active imaginations play tricks on people's eyes? If the apparition is real, why does Osceola return? Some believers think he wants to remind people of his struggles to save the Seminole lands. Others think he wants to be reunited with his remains. Perhaps he wishes to continue to inspire his people. Whether or not Osceola does visit Castillo de San Marcos, the story tells people about the struggle of the Seminole and about a brave leader. ∎

*If you have been timed while reading this selection, enter your reading time below. Then turn to the Words per Minute table on page 155 and look up your reading speed (words per minute). Enter your reading speed on the graph on page 156.*

READING TIME: Unit 8

_____ : _____
*Minutes*          *Seconds*

# How well did you read?

- *Answer the four types of questions that follow. The directions for each type of question tell you how to mark your answers.*

- *When you have finished all four exercises, check your work by using the answer key on page 151. For each right answer, put a check mark (✔) on the line beside the box. For each wrong answer, write the correct answer on the line.*

- *For scoring each exercise, follow the directions below the questions.*

## A FINDING THE MAIN IDEA

Look at the three statements below. One expresses the main idea of the story you just read. A good main idea statement answers two questions: it tells *who* or *what* is the subject of the story, and it answers the understood question *does what?* or *is what?* Another statement is *too broad,* it is vague and doesn't tell much about the topic of the story. The third statement is *too narrow,* it tells about only one part of the story.

Match the statements with the three answer choices below by writing the letter of each answer in the box in front of the statement it goes with.

**M—Main Idea**   **B—Too Broad**   **N—Too Narrow**

_____ ☐ 1. Osceola, a brave leader of the Seminole, was tricked and captured by General Jesup.

_____ ☐ 2. Some people believe that the head of the Seminole chief Osceola appears above Castillo de San Marcos from time to time.

_____ ☐ 3. The apparition of Seminole chief Osceola attracts and inspires many people who are interested in the history of the chief.

_____ Score 15 points for a correct *M* answer
_____ Score 5 points for each correct *B* or *N* answer
_____ TOTAL SCORE: Finding the Main Idea

## B RECALLING FACTS

How well do you remember the facts in the story you just read?
Put an *x* in the box in front of the correct answer to each of the
multiple choice questions below.

1. When Osceola died he was about
   - ____ ☐ a. thirty-five years old.
   - ____ ☐ b. thirty-seven years old.
   - ____ ☐ c. twenty-five years old.

2. Osceola's father was
   - ____ ☐ a. an English trader.
   - ____ ☐ b. a Creek Indian.
   - ____ ☐ c. a Seminole.

3. Osceola died in
   - ____ ☐ a. Florida.
   - ____ ☐ b. Georgia.
   - ____ ☐ c. South Carolina.

4. The government's war with the Seminole
   - ____ ☐ a. ended in 1837.
   - ____ ☐ b. went on for seven years.
   - ____ ☐ c. ended when Osceola was captured.

5. The Seminole
   - ____ ☐ a. never signed a treaty.
   - ____ ☐ b. eventually surrendered.
   - ____ ☐ c. lost their lands in Florida.

Score 5 points for each correct answer

____ TOTAL SCORE: Recalling Facts

## C MAKING INFERENCES

An inference is a judgment that is made or an idea that is
arrived at based on facts or on information that is given. You
make an inference when you understand something that is *not*
stated directly, but that is *implied*, or suggested by the facts that
are given.

Below are five statements that are judgments or ideas that
have been arrived at from the facts of the story. Write the letter
*C* in the box in front of each statement that is a correct inference. Write the letter *F* in front of each faulty inference.

**C—Correct Inference      F—Faulty Inference**

- ____ ☐ 1. General Jesup honored the rules of war.
- ____ ☐ 2. The Seminole were a stubborn people.
- ____ ☐ 3. The Seminole owned valuable land in Florida.
- ____ ☐ 4. The United States government eventually recognized Osceola as a hero.
- ____ ☐ 5. The Seminole loved war.

Score 5 points for each correct answer

____ TOTAL SCORE: Making Inferences

## D USING WORDS PRECISELY

Each of the numbered sentences below contains an underlined word or phrase from the story you have just read. Under the sentence are three definitions. One has the *same* meaning as the underlined word or phrase, one has *almost the same* meaning, and one has the *opposite* meaning. Match the definitions with the three answer choices by writing the letter that stands for each answer in the box in front of the definition it goes with.

**S—Same     A—Almost the Same     O—Opposite**

1. On that day a tall Indian man stood with his hands clasped behind his back, gazing <u>intently</u> into the waters of a shallow creek.

____ ☐ a. carefully

____ ☐ b. with concentration

____ ☐ c. without concern

2. His body ached with weariness brought on by bouts of yellow fever that <u>sapped</u> his strength.

____ ☐ a. removed

____ ☐ b. increased

____ ☐ c. drained

3. When word of General Jesup's <u>deception</u> got out, the whole country was outraged.

____ ☐ a. lie

____ ☐ b. trickery

____ ☐ c. honesty

4. Without a word, he <u>solemnly</u> shook the hands of his family and friends.

____ ☐ a. lightly

____ ☐ b. sadly

____ ☐ c. ceremoniously

5. In 1866 a fire <u>ravaged</u> part of the museum, and Osceola's head was destroyed.

____ ☐ a. improved

____ ☐ b. destroyed

____ ☐ c. damaged

____ Score 3 points for each correct *S* answer
____ Score 1 point for each correct *A* or *O* answer

____ TOTAL SCORE: Using Words Precisely

● *Enter the four total scores in the spaces below, and add them together to find your Critical Reading Score. Then record your Critical Reading Score on the graph on page 157.*

____ Finding the Main Idea
____ Recalling Facts
____ Making Inferences
____ Using Words Precisely

____ CRITICAL READING SCORE: Unit 8

Visitors to Whaley House might well see more than they bargain for when they tour this historic house in San Diego, California: They might get to see the owners, who died in the early part of the century. They could also meet up with a couple of other insubstantial residents while investigating the kitchen and the grounds. There doesn't seem to be anything to worry about though, as the ghosts just go about their own business. The picture here shows Whaley House around the turn of the century, before it was restored and turned into a museum.

# Whaley House

"Welcome to Whaley House," said June Reading with a smile. It was October 9, 1960, and the guests were a Dr. and Mrs. Kirbey from British Columbia, Canada. June Reading was director of the historic house, which stands as one of the finest remaining examples of early American architecture.

Built in the Old Town section of San Diego, California, in 1857, Whaley House was restored and turned into a historical museum in 1957. It opened to the public in April 1960.

After signing in, the Kirbeys wandered by themselves through the gracious home that San Diego pioneer Thomas Whaley had built for his wife and six children. Downstairs are a parlor, a music room, a library, and the kitchen. A large one-story annex is attached to the first-floor rooms. Upstairs are four large bedrooms.

Mrs. Kirbey loved old houses. In fact, she considered herself something of an expert in early architecture. But in Whaley House she found more than she had bargained for.

"Have you ever noticed anything un-usual about the upstairs?" Mrs. Kirbey asked June Reading, when she had com-pleted her wanderings. "What do you mean?" asked June Reading. "When I started upstairs," Mrs. Kirbey began, "I felt a breeze over my head. I didn't see

anything, but I felt a pressure against me that made it hard to continue up the stairs. Then when I looked into the rooms, I had the feeling that someone was standing behind me. The person was so close I expected a tap on my shoulder!"

At the time, June Reading did not know what to make of this. True, she herself had occasionally heard odd noises, such as the sound of heavy footsteps, but she had never experienced anything like what Mrs. Kirbey had related.

June Reading next led the Kirbeys to the annex, which had once served as the San Diego County Courthouse. When they entered the annex, Mrs. Kirbey stopped dead in her tracks. "Someone is here," she whispered. Neither June Reading nor Dr. Kirbey saw anyone.

"Can you describe what it is you are seeing?" June Reading asked. "I see a small figure, that of a woman who has a swarthy complexion. She is wearing a long, full skirt that reaches to the floor. The skirt appears to be made of calico or gingham cloth, with a small print. She has a kind of cap on her head, dark eyes, and she is wearing gold hoops in her pierced ears. She seems to be staying in this room—living here, I gather. I get the impression we are sort of invading her privacy."

After the Kirbeys left, June Reading pondered long and hard about the inci-dent. Mrs. Kirbey did not seem to be the kind of person who would make up such a story, but could it be that there were actually ghosts in Whaley House?

Baffled by the incident, June Reading tried to forget, but she couldn't, for the sound of footsteps in the house continued. "For the next six months," she later said, "I often found myself going upstairs to see if someone was actually there." No one ever was.

June Reading was not the only person to hear strange noises in Whaley House. Workmen often commented on eerie sounds, and so did several volunteer guides. Eventually, still stranger things began happening.

Starting in October 1962, windows on the upper level of the house would suddenly and inexplicably fly open. June Reading had bolts installed to ensure that the windows would remain shut. They did, but then the burglar alarms began ringing at odd hours.

In the months that followed, Whaley House volunteers reported literally scores of strange occurrences. One volunteer reported hearing music and a woman's voice singing "Home Again." He said he later heard organ music, but when he investigated, he found the music room empty and the organ covered. Another volunteer reported seeing a woman dressed in a hoop skirt. A third told of coming upon "the figure of a man, clad in a frock coat and pantaloons," and a dog "spotted . . . like a fox terrier, that ran with its ears flapping, down the hall and into the dining room." Still others told of seeing a rocking chair rocking for no apparent reason, and of smelling cigar smoke and perfume.

These incidents might well have gone unrecorded had it not been for a local TV personality, Regis Philbin. Believing that the strange goings-on at Whaley House would make an interesting subject for his show, Philbin set up a program that featured himself, Hans Holzer, a well-known ghost hunter, June Reading, and a medium.

On June 25, 1965, Philbin, Holzer, a TV crew, and the medium, an English woman named Sybil Leek, met June Reading at Whaley House. Sybil Leek had been told nothing of the strange occurrences, yet from the first, she said she felt "presences" in the house. She immediately felt drawn to the kitchen. As she was on the way, an apparition presented itself. "A child came down the stairs and I followed her," said Sybil.

Later, on live TV, Sybil Leek appeared to withdraw into a trance. Many mediums try to communicate with spirits by entering into trances. While Sybil was in the trance, a voice quite unlike her own

emanated from her lips. It spoke of four ghosts in Whaley House. One was that of a man who often wore heavy boots, opened windows, and rang bells—Thomas Whaley himself. A second was that of Annabelle, a friend of the Whaleys, who had died at the age of thirteen, of poisoning from some food she had taken from the Whaley House kitchen. The strange voice went on to say that the organ music came from Anna Lannay, Thomas Whaley's wife, who had died in the house in 1913. And who was the fourth ghost? It was that of a man called Yankee Jim Robinson. Unjustly charged with stealing a boat, Yankee Jim was hanged in 1852, on the very site where Whaley House would be built five years later.

So the ghosts of Whaley House now had identities. But *why* were they haunting the house? Well, it's often said in ghost stories that the spirits of people return because they are uneasy, because they have suffered some great injustice, or because they have left something unsettled. Do any of those reasons fit the four ghosts?

Thomas Whaley suffered an injustice. In 1869 he signed a contract with the county of San Diego, agreeing to build an annex onto his house, to be leased by the county as a courthouse. He built the annex, but after two years the county broke its lease. Whaley, understandably furious about the breach of contract, petitioned to be reimbursed for building the annex. The matter was never settled. Mrs. Whaley, it can be presumed, also suffered in this matter.

Yankee Jim suffered an even more profound injustice. He was hanged for a crime he did not commit.

As for the youngster Annabelle, maybe she just liked the Whaleys so much that she didn't want to part from them. During her short life, she spent more time at their house than she did in her own.

Whatever the reasons, the ghostly signs continue in Whaley House. In fact, Whaley House is regarded as one of the most actively haunted houses in the world. People claim that Thomas Whaley roams his house, the odor of his beloved Havana cigars trailing behind him. Organ music and singing are heard, and the fragrance of Mrs. Whaley's violet-scented perfume wafts unaccountably through the air. The apparition of a young girl continues to materialize in the kitchen. And Yankee Jim still reportedly wanders the grounds. ■

*If you have been timed while reading this selection, enter your reading time below. Then turn to the Words per Minute table on page 155 and look up your reading speed (words per minute). Enter your reading speed on the graph on page 156.*

READING TIME: Unit 9

_____ : _____
Minutes         Seconds

# How well did you read?

- *Answer the four types of questions that follow. The directions for each type of question tell you how to mark your answers.*

- *When you have finished all four exercises, check your work by using the answer key on page 151. For each right answer, put a check mark (✔) on the line beside the box. For each wrong answer, write the correct answer on the line.*

- *For scoring each exercise, follow the directions below the questions.*

## A  FINDING THE MAIN IDEA

Look at the three statements below. One expresses the main idea of the story you just read. A good main idea statement answers two questions: it tells *who* or *what* is the subject of the story, and it answers the understood question *does what?* or *is what?* Another statement is *too broad,* it is vague and doesn't tell much about the topic of the story. The third statement is *too narrow,* it tells about only one part of the story.

Match the statements with the three answer choices below by writing the letter of each answer in the box in front of the statement it goes with.

**M—Main Idea    B—Too Broad    N—Too Narrow**

_____ ☐ 1. Many people have reportedly witnessed strange and unexplainable occurrences in Whaley House in California.

_____ ☐ 2. A medium named Sybil Leek claimed to have made contact with a spirit who told of ghosts living in Whaley House.

_____ ☐ 3. Whaley House, a historic house in California, is supposedly actively haunted by four ghosts.

_____ Score 15 points for a correct *M* answer

_____ Score 5 points for each correct *B* or *N* answer

_____ TOTAL SCORE: Finding the Main Idea

## B RECALLING FACTS

How well do you remember the facts in the story you just read?
Put an *x* in the box in front of the correct answer to each of the
multiple choice questions below.

1. The first signs that ghosts occupied Whaley House
   occurred
   ___ ☐ a. shortly after the last owners died.
   ___ ☐ b. just before the house opened as a museum.
   ___ ☐ c. soon after the house was opened to the public.

2. Thomas Whaley built an addition onto his house to
   ___ ☐ a. be used as a courthouse.
   ___ ☐ b. accommodate his growing family.
   ___ ☐ c. be used as an office.

3. In 1969 Whaley House was featured on a TV
   ___ ☐ a. news program.
   ___ ☐ b. variety show.
   ___ ☐ c. talk show.

4. The young girl whose ghost materializes in Whaley
   House was
   ___ ☐ a. a friend of the family.
   ___ ☐ b. a servant in the house.
   ___ ☐ c. the Whaleys' niece.

5. Mrs. Kirbey was
   ___ ☐ a. the acting director of Whaley House.
   ___ ☐ b. a visitor to Whaley House.
   ___ ☐ c. a medium.

Score 5 points for each correct answer

___ TOTAL SCORE: Recalling Facts

## C MAKING INFERENCES

An inference is a judgment that is made or an idea that is
arrived at based on facts or on information that is given. You
make an inference when you understand something that is *not*
stated directly, but that is *implied*, or suggested by the facts that
are given.

Below are five statements that are judgments or ideas that
have been arrived at from the facts of the story. Write the letter
*C* in the box in front of each statement that is a correct inference. Write the letter *F* in front of each faulty inference.

**C—Correct Inference       F—Faulty Inference**

___ ☐ 1. Whaley House had become rundown before
        people decided to turn it into a museum.

___ ☐ 2. Mrs. Kirbey believed in ghosts.

___ ☐ 3. Thomas Whaley was a well-known and respected
        man in San Diego.

___ ☐ 4. Sybil Leek was a fraud.

___ ☐ 5. Annabelle had probably been purposely poisoned
        by someone in the Whaley house.

Score 5 points for each correct answer

___ TOTAL SCORE: Making Inferences

## D USING WORDS PRECISELY

Each of the numbered sentences below contains an underlined word or phrase from the story you have just read. Under the sentence are three definitions. One has the *same* meaning as the underlined word or phrase, one has *almost the same* meaning, and one has the *opposite* meaning. Match the definitions with the three answer choices by writing the letter that stands for each answer in the box in front of the definition it goes with.

**S—Same**     **A—Almost the Same**     **O—Opposite**

1. True, she herself had occasionally heard odd noises, such as the sound of heavy footsteps, but she had never experienced anything like what Mrs. Kirbey had <u>related</u>.

____ ☐ a. told about

____ ☐ b. kept secret

____ ☐ c. explained

2. After the Kirbeys left, June Reading <u>pondered</u> long and hard about the incident.

____ ☐ a. thought

____ ☐ b. ignored

____ ☐ c. wondered

3. While Sybil was in the trance, a voice quite unlike her own <u>emanated</u> from her lips.

____ ☐ a. came forth

____ ☐ b. burst

____ ☐ c. became trapped

4. Whaley, understandably furious about the breach of contract, <u>petitioned</u> to be reimbursed for building the annex.

____ ☐ a. demanded

____ ☐ b. asked formally

____ ☐ c. inquired

5. Yankee Jim suffered an even more <u>profound</u> injustice.

____ ☐ a. slight

____ ☐ b. great

____ ☐ c. harsh

____ Score 3 points for each correct *S* answer

____ Score 1 point for each correct *A* or *O* answer

____ TOTAL SCORE: Using Words Precisely

● *Enter the four total scores in the spaces below, and add them together to find your Critical Reading Score. Then record your Critical Reading Score on the graph on page 157.*

_____ Finding the Main Idea
_____ Recalling Facts
_____ Making Inferences
_____ Using Words Precisely
_____ CRITICAL READING SCORE: Unit 9

# The Marine Lieutenant's Ghost

Sometime between eight thirty and nine o'clock on the evening of October 12, 1907, Mrs. Sidney Bartlett was sitting in the living room of her West Coast home when she felt a sudden blow to her head. The strange thing was that nothing and no one visible had struck her. Although she could never explain why, Mrs. Bartlett was convinced that the blow was a message: her son Thomas was in terrible trouble. "Something has happened to Tommy!" she cried out.

The other members of the Bartlett family who were home at the time were startled by Mrs. Bartlett's cry. They were also skeptical of her explanation for it. There was no reason to believe that Thomas, a second lieutenant in the Marine Corps, was in trouble. Although he was stationed on the opposite coast, near the Naval Academy at Annapolis, Maryland, he kept in touch. The last time they had heard from him he sounded fine.

Mrs. Bartlett was unable to sleep that night. A devout Catholic, she prayed for her son's safety. She continued her prayers at mass the next morning, but was so upset she had to leave church early.

At about one thirty that afternoon, the Bartletts received a telephone call. Mr. Bartlett answered the phone and immediately left the house without an explanation. When he returned an hour later, Mrs. Bartlett, who was in another room with her daughter Shirley, saw Thomas walk through the front door behind her husband. "Tommy's here!" she said to Shirley.

By that time Shirley was at her wit's end. She was sure that her mother was having delusions. But Mrs. Bartlett stood by her story. "Tommy is here," she said firmly.

Unaware of their conversation, and looking grim, Mr. Bartlett entered the room and asked, "Can you stand bad news?" Then he told them that he had gone out to pick up a telegram from the navy. He read it aloud to them: "It is reported from Annapolis that Lieutenant Thomas L. Bartlett committed suicide at 1:20 this morning, October 13, 1907."

Mrs. Bartlett couldn't believe her ears. She knew that her son would never commit suicide, which Catholics consider a terrible crime. Then she looked up and saw Thomas standing in front of her.

"Mamma, I never did," he said, reaching his hands toward her. "My hands are as free from crime as they were when I was five years old. Oh, Mother, don't believe them. Case struck me in the head with the butt of a gun and stunned me. I fell on my knees and they beat me worse than a dog in the street. Mamma, dear, if you could only see my forehead you would know what they did to me. Don't give way, for you must clear my name. God will give you the means to bring those men to justice."

Mrs. Bartlett looked at her husband and daughter as if to say, Now do you believe me? But they seemed unaware of Thomas's presence. "Listen," she said, "he is here and I hear him." According to Mrs. Bartlett, her son continued his story this way: "Mamma, they beat me almost to death. I did not know I was shot until my soul went into eternity. They either knocked or struck me in the jaw, for there is a lump on the left side. I never had a chance to defend myself. They broke my watch with a kick as I lay on the ground. They jumped on me with their feet, and I wonder that my ribs were not broken."

Although Mrs. Bartlett repeated these words to her family, they were sure she was just suffering from shock. No one else saw or heard the ghost of Thomas Bartlett.

Mrs. Bartlett claimed that her son's ghost stayed with her for four days. During that time he repeated his version of the story over and over again. He also talked about a man named Hill who, he said, was the leader of his two murderers. Thomas's last words before finally leaving were, "Mamma, don't lose your mind because you've got to clear my name."

Some nights later, Thomas's ghost awakened Mrs. Bartlett. "Don't move," he said. "I am permitted to show you my face." Mrs. Bartlett looked at her son's face and saw that it was badly bruised. Then Thomas asked her to trace the gun found by his body. He said it was not his. He also mentioned that he'd lost a shoulder knot from his uniform.

By that time other members of the Bartlett family had also had some strange experiences. The night after the telegram was received, one of the Bartlett daughters had a dream in which she clearly saw a face—as if she were looking at a photograph. A voice told her that it was the face of the man who had killed Thomas. Later, while reading a newspaper, she saw a photograph of the man in her dream. The newspaper identified the man as Lieutenant Hill.

Thomas's brother, who was at the U.S. Military Academy at West Point, said he saw Thomas in a dream. A married sister dreamed she saw Thomas and heard him say that he had been murdered.

After Thomas's funeral, his belongings were sent to his parents. Among them was his uniform coat, which was missing a shoulder knot, and a watch with a shattered crystal.

Mrs. Bartlett took the watch, held it up, and said, "Tommy is here; listen to his watch ticking." Although her daughter, the only other person in the room, could hear nothing, Mrs. Bartlett was insistent. The watch continued to tick for three minutes, she said, adding that "Tommy says that's how long he suffered." Then she said that the ticking immediately began again. That time the watch ran for two minutes, stopping at twenty minutes after one. Mrs. Bartlett claimed she heard her son say, "That's how much longer I lived." When the watched was repaired, Thomas's brother at West Point carried it. He said that for years it would stop at twenty minutes after one.

The ghost's many appearances to the Bartlett family had convinced them that Thomas Bartlett had not committed suicide. At Mrs. Bartlett's insistence, the navy reopened the case in July, nine months after Thomas's death. At the court hearing, the story that the navy gave was that Thomas and two other officers were returning to their quarters after a dance at the Naval Academy when Thomas, who had been drinking, picked a fight and threatened to kill the others. He went to his quarters and returned with two pistols. When the other two officers tried to get the pistols away from him and arrest

*"Mamma, I never did," cried the anguished ghost of the young marine lieutenant. "Don't give way, for you must clear my name." Mrs. Bartlett's heart grieved for the bruised and battered apparition that was the ghost of her son. And she vowed to help him gain peace. For years she tried to get at the truth and to clear her son's name, but persuading military officials to admit to something that made officers of the United States Marine Corps look bad was not an easy job.*

him, Thomas shot himself in the head.

It was obvious to Mrs. Bartlett that the navy had accepted that story in order to avoid bad publicity. It would certainly not do the navy any good if word got out that two marine officers had turned on a comrade and brutally killed him. Blaming Thomas for his own death was the easiest way out of a nasty situation. Nevertheless, Mrs. Bartlett was unable to prove that her son had been murdered.

Still, she would not give up. At the hearing, three navy doctors had sworn that Thomas's face showed no signs of a beating. Mrs. Bartlett was determined to see the body for herself. Twenty-three months after Thomas's burial, his mother had his body exhumed. When she examined his head, she found all the wounds to be just as Thomas's ghost had described them. Here at last was solid proof! What's more, when Mrs. Bartlett traced the weapon that had killed Thomas, she found that it was a .38 caliber revolver. Thomas's gun had been a .32.

In September of 1910, Mrs. Bartlett wrote a letter to Dr. James H. Hyslop describing Thomas's death and the family's experiences with Thomas's ghost. Dr. Hyslop was then a professor at Columbia University in New York City and the leader of psychical research in the United States. Intrigued by Mrs. Bartlett's story, Dr. Hyslop asked a friend, George A. Thacher, to investigate the details. After three months of careful investigation, Thacher gave his findings to Dr. Hyslop. Based on those findings, Hyslop wrote a detailed report that appeared in a medical journal in 1911. His conclusion: Lieutenant Thomas Bartlett's death was not a suicide, but murder.

Unfortunately, the journal in which Dr. Hyslop's article was published was not widely read. Few people saw the report. What's more, it was published four years after Thomas Bartlett's death. By that time the public had largely forgotten about the tragedy. Much to the Bartlett family's dismay, the article failed to stir up any interest. Yet all the evidence pointed to a huge cover-up by the navy. To this day, the official navy report calls Lieutenant Thomas Bartlett's death a suicide. ■

Note: Some of the names in this story have been changed at the request of those involved.

*If you have been timed while reading this selection, enter your reading time below. Then turn to the Words per Minute table on page 155 and look up your reading speed (words per minute). Enter your reading speed on the graph on page 156.*

| READING TIME: Unit 10 |
| --- |
| _____ : _____ |
| *Minutes*      *Seconds* |

# How well did you read?

- *Answer the four types of questions that follow. The directions for each type of question tell you how to mark your answers.*

- *When you have finished all four exercises, check your work by using the answer key on page 151. For each right answer, put a check mark (✔) on the line beside the box. For each wrong answer, write the correct answer on the line.*

- *For scoring each exercise, follow the directions below the questions.*

## A FINDING THE MAIN IDEA

Look at the three statements below. One expresses the main idea of the story you just read. A good main idea statement answers two questions: it tells *who* or *what* is the subject of the story, and it answers the understood question *does what?* or *is what?* Another statement is *too broad*, it is vague and doesn't tell much about the topic of the story. The third statement is *too narrow*, it tells about only one part of the story.

Match the statements with the three answer choices below by writing the letter of each answer in the box in front of the statement it goes with.

**M—Main Idea     B—Too Broad     N—Too Narrow**

_____ ☐ 1. The ghost of Marine Lieutenant Thomas Bartlett tried to challenge the word of the United States Navy.

_____ ☐ 2. The ghost of Marine Lieutenant Thomas Bartlett, who the navy said had committed suicide, appeared to his mother to tell her that he had been murdered and to ask her to clear his name.

_____ ☐ 3. The ghost of Thomas Bartlett claimed that he had been killed by two fellow officers.

_____ Score 15 points for a correct *M* answer

_____ Score 5 points for each correct *B* or *N* answer

_____ TOTAL SCORE: Finding the Main Idea

## B RECALLING FACTS

How well do you remember the facts in the story you just read? Put an *x* in the box in front of the correct answer to each of the multiple choice questions below.

1. Tom Bartlett had been stationed
   - ___ ☐ a. near the Naval Academy in Annapolis, Maryland.
   - ___ ☐ b. in Washington, D.C.
   - ___ ☐ c. at West Point, New York.

2. The Bartlett family lived
   - ___ ☐ a. in Annapolis, Maryland.
   - ___ ☐ b. on the West Coast.
   - ___ ☐ c. at West Point, New York.

3. Thomas Bartlett was
   - ___ ☐ a. shot to death.
   - ___ ☐ b. stabbed to death.
   - ___ ☐ c. beaten to death.

4. The two men whom the ghost of Thomas Bartlett named as Thomas's murderers were
   - ___ ☐ a. Hyslop and Hill.
   - ___ ☐ b. Hyslop and Thacher.
   - ___ ☐ c. Hill and Case.

5. The gun that was used to kill Thomas was a
   - ___ ☐ a. .38.
   - ___ ☐ b. .22.
   - ___ ☐ c. .45.

Score 5 points for each correct answer

___ TOTAL SCORE: Recalling Facts

## C MAKING INFERENCES

An inference is a judgment that is made or an idea that is arrived at based on facts or on information that is given. You make an inference when you understand something that is *not* stated directly, but that is *implied,* or suggested by the facts that are given.

Below are five statements that are judgments or ideas that have been arrived at from the facts of the story. Write the letter *C* in the box in front of each statement that is a correct inference. Write the letter *F* in front of each faulty inference.

**C—Correct Inference    F—Faulty Inference**

- ___ ☐ 1. The ghost of Thomas Bartlett appeared only to members of the Bartlett family.

- ___ ☐ 2. The navy wanted only to find out the truth about Thomas Bartlett's death.

- ___ ☐ 3. Thomas Bartlett was ashamed of the way he died.

- ___ ☐ 4. Mrs. Bartlett never stopped trying to prove that her son had been murdered.

- ___ ☐ 5. Dr. Hyslop did not appeal to the navy to reopen the case of Thomas Bartlett's death.

Score 5 points for each correct answer

___ TOTAL SCORE: Making Inferences

## D USING WORDS PRECISELY

Each of the numbered sentences below contains an underlined word or phrase from the story you have just read. Under the sentence are three definitions. One has the *same* meaning as the underlined word or phrase, one has *almost the same* meaning, and one has the *opposite* meaning. Match the definitions with the three answer choices by writing the letter that stands for each answer in the box in front of the definition it goes with.

**S—Same**     **A—Almost the Same**     **O—Opposite**

1. A <u>devout</u> Catholic, she prayed for her son's safety.

____ ☐ a. devoted

____ ☐ b. slack

____ ☐ c. strong

2. She was sure that her mother was having <u>delusions</u>.

____ ☐ a. illusions

____ ☐ b. true visions

____ ☐ c. false beliefs

3. Unaware of their conversation, and looking <u>grim</u>, Mr. Bartlett entered the room and asked, "Can you stand bad news?"

____ ☐ a. serious

____ ☐ b. gloomy

____ ☐ c. cheerful

4. Twenty-three months after Thomas's burial, his mother had his body <u>exhumed</u>.

____ ☐ a. dug up

____ ☐ b. buried

____ ☐ c. moved

5. Much to the Bartlett family's <u>dismay</u>, the article failed to stir up any interest.

____ ☐ a. disappointment

____ ☐ b. satisfaction

____ ☐ c. discouragement

____ Score 3 points for each correct *S* answer
____ Score 1 point for each correct *A* or *O* answer

____ TOTAL SCORE: Using Words Precisely

● *Enter the four total scores in the spaces below, and add them together to find your Critical Reading Score. Then record your Critical Reading Score on the graph on page 157.*

_____ Finding the Main Idea
_____ Recalling Facts
_____ Making Inferences
_____ Using Words Precisely

_____ CRITICAL READING SCORE: Unit 10

# The Haunted Gold Mine

A little over a hundred years ago, North Carolina experienced a gold rush that saw men flock to the area between Charlotte and Concord in search of their fortunes. Among the gold seekers was a man with the unlikely name of Skinflint MacIntosh.

It was his reputation as a miser that earned him the name Skinflint. He was so tight that even his body had taken on a pinched and stingy appearance. Local folk claimed he was so skinny that if you looked at him from the side you couldn't see him. Neither the nickname nor the jokes bothered Skinflint, though, for he owned one of the richest gold mines in North Carolina.

Skinflint did have one problem: finding men willing to dig his treasure. You see, the gold in Skinflint's mine lay some 450 feet down. In most of the other mines, the gold was close to the surface, making it easier to get at. The deeper the gold, the more dangerous the job of dragging it out of the earth. The farther down tunnels had to be dug to reach the prize, the more tons of dirt and rock that had to be supported with wooden beams. Those beams were all that stood between the burrowing miners and death by suffocation. It took men of extraordinary skill and courage to work the MacIntosh Mine. Skinflint set out to find just such miners.

He sent word that anyone willing to work his mine would be paid half again what other mine owners were paying. Nevertheless, to his surprise, there were no takers. A miner named Joe McGee spoke for all the others when he explained, "Who wants to go that far down to dig? No amount of money is worth working for if a man dies before he can collect it."

The other miners nodded in agreement, because Joe McGee knew more about mining than anyone else. He was the top foreman at the Reed Mine, probably the richest lode in North Carolina.

Refusing to concede, MacIntosh asserted, "It doesn't matter how deep a mine is. I make sure my tunnels are held up by good heavy timber. Why, since I got the mine, I've been down in it more times than I can count, and I'm still here ain't I?"

Now Skinflint MacIntosh was hardly the most popular man in town, but he did have a way with words. The miners had to admit MacIntosh had a point. In fact, even Joe McGee looked interested. "Mr. MacIntosh," he said, "if your mine is so safe, then there's no more danger working it than any other mine, right?" "Positively, Joe," MacIntosh answered, a convincing smile on his face. "I'll work for you then," Joe said, "but if I get buried in your mine, I want you to pay my wife one thousand dollars."

In those days a thousand dollars was considered a barrel of money, yet without batting an eyelash, MacIntosh agreed. "Joe," he said, "I'm so sure my mine is safe, I'll pay her *two* thousand!"

That very day, Joe quit his job at the Reed Mine. Lured by the promise of high wages, a dozen other miners followed him. With a complete crew, it wasn't long before Skinflint was watching great quantities of ore being hauled from his mine.

At first Jennie McGee worried about her husband's safety, but when he came home whistling cheerfully night after night, her fears lessened. "I wouldn't leave you and the baby," Joe assured her.

Then one night Joe didn't show up for supper. At first Jennie made excuses about snow, which was falling heavily, but when Joe had not arrived by nine o'clock, Jennie grew frantic. She bundled the baby in blankets and hurried to the local saloon, reasoning that Joe might have stopped to have a drink with some friends, though it wasn't his way to do such a thing without letting her know. He wasn't there, and no one had seen him. Jennie then dashed to the home of Joe's best friend, Shaun O'Hennessy.

"It's late for you to be out in such weather, Jennie," Shaun chided, drawing her inside. When Jennie explained that she was looking for Joe, Shaun frowned. "I waited for him after work, but he said he was staying on for a while." "Oh, Shaun," Jennie cried, "I just know something horrible has happened. Please go back to the mine and look for him!" "You return home, Jennie," Shaun answered gently, "and I'll get to the mine as soon as I can."

On his way, Shaun rounded up several other miners to assist him. When the group reached the mine shaft, Shaun and one other miner clambered down the ladders, passing old tunnels, until they reached the vein where the men had been working that day. Using lanterns to illuminate the way, they searched every inch of the tunnel, but there was no sign of Joe McGee.

When Jennie heard the news, she refused to believe that her husband was not trapped somewhere in the mine. The next day she pleaded with Skinflint MacIntosh to send a search party into the older tunnels to look for her husband. MacIntosh refused to help, saying that he was convinced Joe was in hiding—that he would appear "in his own good time."

Two weeks went by, and Jennie paid MacIntosh another visit. Convinced that her husband had perished in the mine, she had gone to claim the money MacIntosh

had promised. "Know what I believe?" MacIntosh offered, eyeing Jennie shrewdly. "I think Joe simply tuckered of married life and he vamoosed." "But Joe loved me and the baby—I'm positive he did," Jennie insisted. "Then wait awhile longer," MacIntosh argued.

*Checking the safety of a mine, as workers are doing in the Reed Gold Mine, below, is standard procedure today. But in the mid-1800s, mining was a risky proposition. Loading ore into buckets called kibbles to be hauled to the surface, miners labored in deep tunnels supported by wooden beams that were seldom checked for weaknesses. In the bowels of the MacIntosh Mine, Joe McGee fell victim to rotten supports. But he swore that death would not keep him from getting revenge. Skinflint MacIntosh would pay.*

But Jennie was running out of time. She had little money and was low on firewood and food. Finally she steeled herself for yet another visit to MacIntosh. This time, however, he refused to see her.

That night, Shaun O'Hennessy was awakened by a persistent knocking on his front door. When he opened it, he was confronted by a horrible vision. A man, or what had once been a man, stared at him from blood-red eyes sunken deeply into blackened sockets. The visage the apparition wore was deadly white. Its clothes were tattered and encrusted with dirt.

"Shaun O'Hennessy," the apparition moaned, "how could you, my best friend, abandon me to that mine?" Unable to believe that this ghastly thing was the spirit of Joe McGee, Shaun stood speechless.

"You searched too deep, Shaun," the spirit continued. "You must look for me in the second tunnel." Shaun whispered hoarsely, "I'll find you, Joe, I swear I will!" "Did Jennie get the money Skinflint promised?" "No," Shaun answered, "he insists you're not dead, Joe—that you ran away." "I'll get that liar," vowed the ghost of Joe McGee, "and I'll haunt his mine forever."

That night Shaun again rounded up miners to search for the body of Joe McGee, and that time he knew exactly where to look. Deep inside the second tunnel, a voice floated out of the darkness: "I've been waiting for you, boys." In the light of their lanterns, the men recognized the terrible apparition that was Joe McGee.

"Skinflint MacIntosh was a liar," the voice continued. "The timbers in this mine are so rotten no one is safe." Then pointing to a great mound of dirt, the apparition said, "This is where I was buried." Sure enough, after some frantic digging, the miners uncovered Joe McGee's body.

The following day, Shaun went to Skinflint MacIntosh and announced, "Joe's back, and he needs to see you about some important business." MacIntosh appeared startled, but he followed Shaun to Joe's house, where a group of miners and their wives had gathered. Grave eyes followed as Shaun led MacIntosh through the entryway and over to a rough pine box. Jennie, holding her baby, sat rocking quietly next to the coffin.

"A thousand dollars, that's what I agreed to," MacIntosh sputtered, looking down at Joe McGee's body. "It was *two* thousand," Shaun contradicted, "and there are plenty of witnesses to back me up." Realizing he was beaten, MacIntosh muttered, "All right, his widow can pick it up at my office." Then he turned and hurried out the door. Jennie got her money, but it was small compensation for the husband she missed so terribly.

After Joe's funeral, MacIntosh expected work at the mine to start up again, but the miners refused to return. Skinflint had lied about the safety of the mine, and he had tried to cheat Jennie out of her money. What is more, the ghost of Joe McGee had promised to haunt the mine forever, and no one wanted to work in a haunted mine.

A few weeks later MacIntosh went to the mine and just sat, aimlessly running the red Carolina clay through his fingers. As he sat and sifted and contemplated the turn of events, he got madder and madder. Finally, old Skinflint lost his mind completely. He was discovered on his knees, clawing at the earth, tears streaming down his face and animal wails pouring from his lips.

Well, Skinflint's gold is still there, deep under the red clay, waiting for some brave souls to dig it out. Legend has it that Joe McGee, true to his word, haunts the mine that took his life. Should you visit the site and stand quietly listening, you might hear the wind whisper the names of the famous Carolina mines of the gold rush era. You will hear Dixie Queen, Yellow Dog, Blue Hill, Dutch Bend, and Reed. But you will never hear the name MacIntosh. The ghost of Joe McGee, it is said, will not permit it. ■

*If you have been timed while reading this selection, enter your reading time below. Then turn to the Words per Minute table on page 155 and look up your reading speed (words per minute). Enter your reading speed on the graph on page 156.*

READING TIME: Unit 11

_____ : _____
*Minutes*        *Seconds*

# How well did you read?

- *Answer the four types of questions that follow. The directions for each type of question tell you how to mark your answers.*

- *When you have finished all four exercises, check your work by using the answer key on page 150. For each right answer, put a check mark (✔) on the line beside the box. For each wrong answer, write the correct answer on the line.*

- *For scoring each exercise, follow the directions below the questions.*

## A FINDING THE MAIN IDEA

Look at the three statements below. One expresses the main idea of the story you just read. A good main idea statement answers two questions: it tells *who* or *what* is the subject of the story, and it answers the understood question *does what?* or *is what?* Another statement is *too broad,* it is vague and doesn't tell much about the topic of the story. The third statement is *too narrow,* it tells about only one part of the story.

Match the statements with the three answer choices below by writing the letter of each answer in the box in front of the statement it goes with.

**M—Main Idea**   **B—Too Broad**   **N—Too Narrow**

____ ☐ 1. A ghost in the MacIntosh Mine kept workers away and pushed the owner to insanity and financial ruin.

____ ☐ 2. Joe McGee was killed in the MacIntosh Mine because of Skinflint MacIntosh's stingy, uncaring ways.

____ ☐ 3. Joe McGee, killed in the MacIntosh Mine because of the owner's cheap ways, haunted the mine to bring Skinflint MacIntosh to ruin.

____ Score 15 points for a correct *M* answer

____ Score 5 points for each correct *B* or *N* answer

____ TOTAL SCORE: Finding the Main Idea

## B  RECALLING FACTS

How well do you remember the facts in the story you just read?
Put an x in the box in front of the correct answer to each of the
multiple choice questions below.

1. The MacIntosh Mine is in
   - ___ ☐ a. Tennessee.
   - ___ ☐ b. North Carolina.
   - ___ ☐ c. California.

2. Joe McGee offered to work the MacIntosh Mine if
   Skinflint would
   - ___ ☐ a. pay all the miners twice what other mines
     were paying.
   - ___ ☐ b. agree to pay his wife a thousand dollars if he
     was killed in the mine.
   - ___ ☐ c. make sure all the supports in the mine
     were strong.

3. Jennie was
   - ___ ☐ a. glad that Joe was working for MacIntosh.
   - ___ ☐ b. comforted by the money that MacIntosh gave
     her after Joe's death.
   - ___ ☐ c. worried about Joe working in the
     MacIntosh Mine.

4. Joe McGee's ghost first appeared to
   - ___ ☐ a. Shaun O'Hennessy.
   - ___ ☐ b. his wife, Jennie.
   - ___ ☐ c. Skinflint MacIntosh.

5. MacIntosh eventually paid Jennie
   - ___ ☐ a. a thousand dollars.
   - ___ ☐ b. two thousand dollars.
   - ___ ☐ c. nothing.

Score 5 points for each correct answer

___ TOTAL SCORE: Recalling Facts

## C  MAKING INFERENCES

An inference is a judgment that is made or an idea that is
arrived at based on facts or on information that is given. You
make an inference when you understand something that is *not*
stated directly, but that is *implied,* or suggested by the facts that
are given.

Below are five statements that are judgments or ideas that
have been arrived at from the facts of the story. Write the letter
*C* in the box in front of each statement that is a correct inference. Write the letter *F* in front of each faulty inference.

**C—Correct Inference    F—Faulty Inference**

- ___ ☐ 1. Skinflint MacIntosh respected Joe McGee.
- ___ ☐ 2. The MacIntosh Mine was the only mine in the
  area ever to have a fatal cave-in.
- ___ ☐ 3. Joe McGee was a heavy drinker.
- ___ ☐ 4. Skinflint MacIntosh didn't care that Joe McGee
  died.
- ___ ☐ 5. If Joe McGee had not agreed to work for
  MacIntosh, Skinflint probably would not have
  been able to work his mine.

Score 5 points for each correct answer

___ TOTAL SCORE: Making Inferences

## D USING WORDS PRECISELY

Each of the numbered sentences below contains an underlined word or phrase from the story you have just read. Under the sentence are three definitions. One has the *same* meaning as the underlined word or phrase, one has *almost the same* meaning, and one has the *opposite* meaning. Match the definitions with the three answer choices by writing the letter that stands for each answer in the box in front of the definition it goes with.

**S—Same    A—Almost the Same    O—Opposite**

1. Refusing to <u>concede</u>, MacIntosh asserted, "It doesn't matter how deep a mine is."

____ ☐ a. argue

____ ☐ b. agree

____ ☐ c. accept

2. "Know what I believe?" MacIntosh offered, eyeing Jennie <u>shrewdly</u>.

____ ☐ a. kindly

____ ☐ b. slyly

____ ☐ c. sharply

3. Finally she <u>steeled</u> herself for yet another visit to MacIntosh.

____ ☐ a. readied

____ ☐ b. braced

____ ☐ c. relaxed

4. "It was *two* thousand," Shaun <u>contradicted</u>, "and there are plenty of witnesses to back me up."

____ ☐ a. denied

____ ☐ b. disagreed

____ ☐ c. confirmed

5. Jennie got her money, but it was small <u>compensation</u> for the husband she missed so terribly.

____ ☐ a. cost

____ ☐ b. payment

____ ☐ c. satisfaction

____ Score 3 points for each correct *S* answer
____ Score 1 point for each correct *A* or *O* answer

____ TOTAL SCORE: Using Words Precisely

● *Enter the four total scores in the spaces below, and add them together to find your Critical Reading Score. Then record your Critical Reading Score on the graph on page 157.*

____ Finding the Main Idea
____ Recalling Facts
____ Making Inferences
____ Using Words Precisely

____ **CRITICAL READING SCORE: Unit 11**

# Sarah's Ghost House

In 1862 Sarah Pardee had everything to look forward to. That year she married William Wirt Winchester, heir to the Winchester rifle fortune. (At that time the Winchester rifle was the most famous rifle in the world.) Sarah and her husband moved to a large, lovely home in New Haven, Connecticut. Soon they had a baby girl, whom they named Annie Pardee. Then tragedy struck. Just one month after her birth, baby Annie died from a mysterious illness. A few short months later, William also died.

Sarah was devastated. She withdrew into her home and refused to see anyone. She thought only of her double tragedy, and became convinced that the Winchesters were cursed. The rifle that bore their name had been responsible for the deaths of thousands. Sarah felt that the spirits of those dead people were seeking revenge.

Sarah had always been interested in the occult—the mysteries of the spirit world. Now she became obsessed with it. Hoping to make contact with her baby and her husband, Sarah invited mediums into her home. Mediums claim that they can contact the dead through meetings called séances. None of the mediums, however, was able to get through to William or to baby Annie.

Then Sarah learned of a medium named Adam Coons, who lived in Boston. People assured her that if anyone could make contact with the dead, he could. Without telling him who she was, Sarah visited Coons, and he agreed to stage a séance for her.

During the séance, Coons told Sarah that the spirit of her late husband was standing beside her. "Tell him that I miss him desperately," she said. "He wants you to know that he will always be with you," Coons replied. Then he gave Sarah a chilling warning. "Unless you do something in their memory, the ghosts of those who have been killed by Winchester rifles will haunt you forever."

"But what can I do?" Sarah pleaded. Coons told her that she was to move to the West and buy a house that her husband's spirit would pick out. Then she was to enlarge the house, making sure it had enough room to house those spirits. As long as she continued to build on to the house, Sarah was told, she would remain alive and unharmed.

Coons had not been told Sarah's identity. How, then, did he know about her husband's death and the family's connection to the Winchester rifle? Sarah was convinced that the ghost of her husband had spoken through the medium. She set out to follow his instructions.

In 1884 Sarah sold her home in New Haven and traveled to California. There, following what she later said was William's advice, she bought an eight-room house on forty-four acres of land in San Jose, a city about fifty miles south of San Francisco.

She set about enlarging the house. Luckily, money was no problem. Sarah had inherited William's fortune—about twenty million dollars. She also received about a thousand dollars a day from the Winchester Arms Company.

Sarah hired a small army of workers. There were eighteen carpenters, twelve gardeners, and countless plumbers, plasterers, stonemasons, and painters. For the next thirty-eight years, they worked around the clock, every day, all year long. The hammering and sawing never ceased.

Sarah herself took charge of every detail of the work. Each morning she gave the head workman the plans she had sketched on an old envelope or paper bag the night before. And each night she would seek the opinions of the ghosts that she said inhabited the house. More often than not, it seems, they did not like her plans, or they would change their minds about what they wanted.

The result was that walls built one day would be torn down the next. Windows would be installed only to be blocked up. Doors were added, then taken out, and so on. One worker spent thirty-three years doing nothing but laying fancy wooden floors and then tearing them up!

As each new room was completed, Sarah would furnish it or fill it with treasures that would later be used to furnish other rooms. Some rooms held rolls of costly French wallpapers. Others held stacks of paintings. Still others were crammed with ornaments of copper, gold, and silver.

Railroad cars filled with European and Asian riches for the mansion arrived almost daily at the San Jose depot. For small items, Sarah shopped locally. She drove one of her two automobiles—both two-tone lavender and yellow Pierce Arrows. When she arrived at a store, she never got out of the car. No matter, for the eager shopkeepers gladly brought items out for her approval.

Sarah spent almost as much time planning the grounds as she did the house. She ordered her gardeners to plant a six-foot-high cypress hedge around the entire estate. They also planted exotic gardens and orchards. Elaborate fountains spewed water twenty-four hours a day. And paths wound through this wonderland in a confusing maze.

In honor of the many Indians killed by

*Why would anyone build a 160-room house sprawling over six acres of land and live in it alone—no visitors allowed? Sarah Winchester did it out of fear and a desire to live forever. And she didn't consider herself alone in the house. In addition to her servants, she had the company of a good number of ghosts. It is believed that the many skylights in the house were built to let out the shadows of evil spirits. Sarah tried to encourage only friendly ghosts.*

white armies using Winchester rifles, Sarah had a statue sculpted for the garden. It depicted Chief Little Fawn shooting arrows.

In the end, the house covered six acres. It contained 160 rooms, 47 fireplaces, and 40 staircases. There were 10,000 windows, 52 skylights, 467 doorways, 6 kitchens, a formal dining room, and a grand ball-room. In all, Sarah spent five million dollars on her ghost house.

Some details of the house are quite odd. It has five heating systems and three elevators. Secret passageways are everywhere, but many lead to blank walls. Many of the staircases lead nowhere. One has forty steps, each only two inches high! One room has nothing but trap doors. Another has a skylight—in the floor. On the second floor, some of the doors open onto thin air.

Sarah was obsessed by the number thirteen. Each light fixture has thirteen globes. Some stairs have thirteen steps. The house has thirteen bathrooms, and Sarah's bathroom has thirteen windows.

The house took up Sarah's every waking moment. The work was *all* she had, for she never invited anyone into the house. Even a president was turned away from the door. In 1903 President Theodore Roosevelt dropped by for a visit but was told by a servant that "the house was not open to strangers." He never did get in.

But perhaps Sarah was not alone in her rambling mansion. In later years, it was said that every night, when the tower bell tolled midnight, organ music wafted from the house. It could not have been Sarah playing, for her fingers had grown so stiff with age that she could hardly hold a pencil.

Clearly, Sarah herself believed that she had ghostly guests, for she dined with them each evening. Servants would set thirteen places at the table, heap each plate with food, and fill the crystal goblets with the finest wines. That was Sarah's nightly offering to any spirits who cared to dine. "Good evening," she would say. "I am pleased that you have come to share my food and my house. Please enjoy yourselves." Early each morning, the servants would clear the dining room. They never revealed whether the food and wine had been touched.

Outwardly, Sarah was the perfect hostess, but secretly she was terrified of the ghosts. So that they wouldn't find her when she was sleeping, she slept in a different room each night.

Sarah Winchester devoted her life to making amends to those who had been killed by Winchester rifles. But the house she labored over was not enough to save her, despite Adam Coons's promise that she would not die as long as she kept building. She died there in 1922, at the age of eighty-five. At the time of her death, there was enough material on the site to continue building for another thirty-eight years.

Sarah left no will, so the furnishings were put up for auction. It took six large vans working eight hours a day for six weeks to haul off all her belongings. A year later the house itself was sold. The new owners opened it to visitors, charging a fee for the opportunity to wander through it. On May 13, 1974, the Winchester House was designated a California Historical Landmark.

Today visitors marvel at the strange, sprawling building. Frequent visitors say that the house is larger today than it was when Sarah died. Since there were no plans for the house, no blueprints, there is no proof. Still, people insist that new rooms have been added. Could Sarah still be trying to make amends? Some people think so. But whatever the case, the Winchester House is like no other house on earth—an architectural fun house built for the comfort of invisible residents. ■

*If you have been timed while reading this selection, enter your reading time below. Then turn to the Words per Minute table on page 155 and look up your reading speed (words per minute). Enter your reading speed on the graph on page 156.*

READING TIME: Unit 12

———— : ————
*Minutes*        *Seconds*

# How well did you read?

- *Answer the four types of questions that follow. The directions for each type of question tell you how to mark your answers.*

- *When you have finished all four exercises, check your work by using the answer key on page 151. For each right answer, put a check mark (✔) on the line beside the box. For each wrong answer, write the correct answer on the line.*

- *For scoring each exercise, follow the directions below the questions.*

## A  FINDING THE MAIN IDEA

Look at the three statements below. One expresses the main idea of the story you just read. A good main idea statement answers two questions: it tells *who* or *what* is the subject of the story, and it answers the understood question *does what?* or *is what?* Another statement is *too broad*, it is vague and doesn't tell much about the topic of the story. The third statement is *too narrow*, it tells about only one part of the story.

Match the statements with the three answer choices below by writing the letter of each answer in the box in front of the statement it goes with.

**M—Main Idea     B—Too Broad     N—Too Narrow**

_____  ☐  1. Sarah Winchester built a huge, unusual house in Southern California.

_____  ☐  2. Sarah Winchester spent most of her life trying to make amends for the deaths of people killed by Winchester rifles.

_____  ☐  3. Sarah Winchester built a huge, rambling puzzle of a house for the ghosts of the people killed by Winchester rifles.

_____  Score 15 points for a correct *M* answer
_____  Score 5 points for each correct *B* or *N* answer
_____  TOTAL SCORE: Finding the Main Idea

## B RECALLING FACTS

How well do you remember the facts in the story you just read? Put an *x* in the box in front of the correct answer to each of the multiple choice questions below.

1. Sarah Winchester moved to San Jose, California, from
   - ____ ☐ a. Boston, Massachusetts.
   - ____ ☐ b. San Francisco, California.
   - ____ ☐ c. New Haven, Connecticut.

2. All her life, Sarah had been interested in
   - ____ ☐ a. rifles.
   - ____ ☐ b. the occult.
   - ____ ☐ c. building a great mansion.

3. Sarah went to mediums in order to
   - ____ ☐ a. try to contact her dead husband and baby.
   - ____ ☐ b. ask the spirits of people killed by Winchester rifles how she might make amends to them.
   - ____ ☐ c. find out what she should do with her life.

4. Sarah started building her mansion in the
   - ____ ☐ a. early 1900s.
   - ____ ☐ b. late 1800s.
   - ____ ☐ c. 1840s.

5. Sarah's house contained
   - ____ ☐ a. 725 rooms.
   - ____ ☐ b. 467 rooms.
   - ____ ☐ c. 160 rooms.

Score 5 points for each correct answer

____ TOTAL SCORE: Recalling Facts

## C MAKING INFERENCES

An inference is a judgment that is made or an idea that is arrived at based on facts or on information that is given. You make an inference when you understand something that is *not* stated directly, but that is *implied,* or suggested by the facts that are given.

Below are five statements that are judgments or ideas that have been arrived at from the facts of the story. Write the letter *C* in the box in front of each statement that is a correct inference. Write the letter *F* in front of each faulty inference.

**C—Correct Inference     F—Faulty Inference**

- ____ ☐ 1. William Winchester was an evil man.

- ____ ☐ 2. Adam Coons continued to advise Sarah Winchester throughout her life.

- ____ ☐ 3. If William and Annie had not died, Sarah would not have built her ghost house.

- ____ ☐ 4. The materials that were left on the site when Sarah died were used to continue adding to the house.

- ____ ☐ 5. Sarah had no friends.

Score 5 points for each correct answer

____ TOTAL SCORE: Making Inferences

## D USING WORDS PRECISELY

Each of the numbered sentences below contains an underlined word or phrase from the story you have just read. Under the sentence are three definitions. One has the *same* meaning as the underlined word or phrase, one has *almost the same* meaning, and one has the *opposite* meaning. Match the definitions with the three answer choices by writing the letter that stands for each answer in the box in front of the definition it goes with.

**S—Same    A—Almost the Same    O—Opposite**

1. Now she became underlined obsessed with it.

___ ☐ a. highly involved

___ ☐ b. totally absorbed

___ ☐ c. uninterested

2. Elaborate fountains spewed water twenty-four hours a day.

___ ☐ a. shot forth

___ ☐ b. pulled in

___ ☐ c. gave off

3. It depicted Chief Little Fawn shooting arrows.

___ ☐ a. demonstrated

___ ☐ b. hid

___ ☐ c. showed

4. Sarah Winchester devoted her life to making amends to those who had been killed by Winchester rifles.

___ ☐ a. making up for

___ ☐ b. apologizing

___ ☐ c. further offending

5. But the house she labored over was not enough to save her, despite Adam Coons's promise that she would not die as long as she kept building.

___ ☐ a. even with

___ ☐ b. regardless of

___ ☐ c. because of

___ Score 3 points for each correct *S* answer

___ Score 1 point for each correct *A* or *O* answer

___ TOTAL SCORE: Using Words Precisely

- *Enter the four total scores in the spaces below, and add them together to find your Critical Reading Score. Then record your Critical Reading Score on the graph on page 157.*

___ Finding the Main Idea
___ Recalling Facts
___ Making Inferences
___ Using Words Precisely

___ CRITICAL READING SCORE: Unit 12

# The Ghost Ship of Georges Bank

A few miles west of Gloucester, Massachusetts, lies the picturesque town of Essex. Now a favorite haunt of antique hunters scouring Boston's North Shore, Essex was once one of the major shipbuilding centers in the country. There was no excitement, therefore, when the fishing schooner *Charles Haskell* was readied for launching one day late in the spring of 1868. The launching of a fishing boat was a routine event.

Indeed, the *Haskell* was nearly identical to hundreds of other vessels of its type already sailing the waters off New England. It had two masts and a deck some one hundred feet long. It had no engine and would carry a crew of about ten fishermen. These sailing vessels were fat and rugged, capable of carrying tons of cod, haddock, and halibut in their spacious holds below decks.

Like others of the same design, the *Haskell* would fish the waters of Georges Bank, the richest fishing grounds in the world. The Bank covers 8,500 square miles of the Atlantic Ocean, about a hundred miles east of Cape Cod.

Georges Bank may be the richest fishing grounds in the world, but it is also one of the most treacherous. In fact, for years many fishermen refused to work those waters. Strong currents slice across the Bank, whose shallow waters seem always to be cold and gray. Dense fog can drop like a heavy curtain, obscuring everything beyond a few feet of one's eyes. Sudden squalls and fierce gales have been known to devastate entire fishing fleets—sending some boats limping home and others plunging to the bottom of the sea. Those were the conditions in which the *Charles Haskell* was built to work. The fate that was to befall it was one that neither its builder nor its owner could have foreseen.

Its eerie tale begins on the evening before the *Haskell* was to be launched. That night a workman inspected the boat, checking to see that all was in readiness for the launch. But as he was making his way around the deck, he tripped and fell through an open hatch. His body was discovered the next morning. He had died of a broken neck.

Now, sailors are nothing if not superstitious, so it was no surprise when the captain who had commissioned the *Haskell* refused to accept the vessel. "A man lies dead on this ship already," he muttered to the builder, "and she has yet to touch the sea. That is a bad omen, and I shall not take her."

The unhappy builder launched the *Haskell* anyway, but it lay at the wharf, unused, for the better part of a year. Then along came Captain Clifford Curtis, who, sensing a bargain, purchased the *Haskell* and took it to Gloucester. Captain Curtis then signed on a crew and set out, on March 6, 1869, for Georges Bank.

No sooner had they reached the Bank than they began to haul in fish as fast as they could man the lines. This will surely be a record catch, Captain Curtis thought, and on the *Haskell*'s first voyage. But that was not to be. Georges Bank was about to give evidence of its notorious fickleness.

Hard at work hauling fish, neither the crew nor Captain Curtis noticed the wind rising. When they finally realized that a storm was building, orders were given crisply and forcefully. "Down sails! Drop anchor! Bring in all fishing lines! Quickly, now, we've a blow coming!"

The captain studied the surrounding waters, noting the locations of the fishing boats nearest them. He had to make certain that the *Haskell* was anchored well away from other schooners in the fleet. Should the boat drag anchor or snap its anchor line, it would career through the fleet, out of control. That could prove disastrous. Satisfied that all was well, Captain Curtis ordered the crew below decks, except for a lone sailor who was charged with watching for runaway vessels.

By nine o'clock that night the winds had grown to hurricane force—more than seventy-five miles per hour. That was when the dreaded call came from the sailor on watch: Sail ho! It was a runaway, and it was headed straight for the *Haskell!*

On deck in an instant, Captain Curtis, ax in hand, rushed to the bow and shattered the anchor chain with one mighty blow. Instantly, the *Haskell* was at the mercy of the shrieking winds.

For nearly half an hour the schooner thundered through the fleet, narrowly missing vessel after vessel. But its luck could not last. The *Haskell* slammed into the *Andrew Johnson,* a schooner out of Salem. Within minutes the *Johnson* had sunk to the bottom, its crew leaping into the roiling waters. The *Haskell,* only slightly damaged, slipped off into the darkness, the awful cries of the doomed *Johnson* sailors lost in the winds.

"Captain," a sailor on the *Haskell* whispered hoarsely, "did you see the terrible look on their faces?" "Aye, lad," came the answer. Then Captain Curtis added quickly, "But there's no blood on our hands, no blood a'tall."

The *Haskell* returned safely to Gloucester, where the crew learned that nine ships had been lost in the storm,

*The* **Charles Haskell** *was an unlucky boat from the start, and men were reluctant to sail on it. But a crew was finally rounded up, and the schooner set out for the rich fishing grounds of Georges Bank. Fishermen willingly faced the natural dangers caused by the sudden storms common on the Bank, but if that crew had known the unnatural fate that awaited them aboard the* **Haskell,** *they would never have set foot on the vessel.*

but only one—the *Andrew Johnson*—had been sunk by another vessel. And all Gloucester and nearby Salem knew the *Haskell* had sunk it.

Once again the *Haskell* lay idle at the wharf for months, while Captain Curtis sought to muster another crew. That proved difficult, however. "She's a Jonah," was the word on the docks. (A Jonah is one who brings misfortune.) "The families of those who sailed on the *Johnson* will not soon forget this incident."

But time passed, people's anger softened, and Captain Curtis eventually got himself a new crew. Shortly thereafter, the *Haskell* set out for its second voyage to Georges Bank.

For five days on the Bank, both the weather and the fishing were ideal. Then, on the sixth day, a typically thick fog settled in and the wind fell off completely, leaving a complete calm.

That night Joe Enos and Harry Richardson stood the deck watch. Within an hour Enos was asleep. His watchmate busied himself looking out for other vessels. Suddenly he jabbed Joe Enos in the ribs. Too frightened to speak, Richardson could only point toward the bow of the boat. There four ghostly figures stood. "Them ain't our men!" Enos shrieked. "Then who . . . or *what* . . . are they?" Richardson asked.

As the two men stood transfixed, six more ghostly figures silently climbed aboard the *Haskell* from the dark waters. Without a word, they went to the rail and began to fish. Other than the creaking of

the wooden vessel as it rolled in the gentle seas, the only sound to be heard was that of the boat's clock sounding eight bells—midnight.

At that moment Captain Curtis stepped on deck. "Look, Captain, do you see 'em?" "I got eyes, ain't I?" Captain Curtis answered gruffly. "But I tell you, there's no blood on our hands." "Captain," Harry Richardson pleaded, "we're seeing the ghosts of the *Johnson*. We must head for home—we *must*! I'll not stay another night, even if I have to swim back to Gloucester!"

The three men began arguing, and the sound of their voices brought the rest of the crew on deck. Not once did any of the apparitions look up or stop fishing at the rail.

Finally the crew won over Captain Curtis. "Get the anchor in," he growled, "we sail for home now." With those words the ghostly figures at the rail disappeared. The very next night, again at midnight, the apparitions returned and once again manned the rails. As if in answer, the *Haskell*'s crew threw up every scrap of sail the ship could carry, in an attempt to move faster.

At dawn, as they neared the entrance to Gloucester Harbor, Captain Curtis took the wheel. When he did, one of the ghosts turned to face him. The apparition stared long and hard at the captain, eyes burning in resentment. Then it slowly shook its head in disgust. With that, it motioned to the other ghosts, and one by one, they

slipped silently over the side into the dark waters. "We have no blood on our hands! No blood . . . I swear it!" Captain Curtis screamed into the early morning light.

Needless to say, the *Charles Haskell* never put out to sea again. It remained at the wharf, slowly rotting, until it was finally towed ashore and destroyed. It is said that as the hulk burned the sighs of the drowned sailors of the *Johnson* were heard rising with the flames, and that the apparitions of ten fishermen rose from the ship and floated off into nothingness. The *Haskell* was dead. The spirits of the men could finally rest.

As for Captain Curtis, well, he could never get anyone to sail with him, so he left town and simply drifted into obscurity. Enos and Richardson and the rest of the *Haskell*'s crew, as far as is known, eventually went back to sea. Fishing was the only life they knew, and Georges Bank was where the fish were. ■

*If you have been timed while reading this selection, enter your reading time below. Then turn to the Words per Minute table on page 155 and look up your reading speed (words per minute). Enter your reading speed on the graph on page 156.*

READING TIME: Unit 13

_____ : _____
Minutes     Seconds

94

# How well did you read?

- *Answer the four types of questions that follow. The directions for each type of question tell you how to mark your answers.*

- *When you have finished all four exercises, check your work by using the answer key on page 151. For each right answer, put a check mark (✔) on the line beside the box. For each wrong answer, write the correct answer on the line.*

- *For scoring each exercise, follow the directions below the questions.*

## A  FINDING THE MAIN IDEA

Look at the three statements below. One expresses the main idea of the story you just read. A good main idea statement answers two questions: it tells *who* or *what* is the subject of the story, and it answers the understood question *does what?* or *is what?* Another statement is *too broad,* it is vague and doesn't tell much about the topic of the story. The third statement is *too narrow,* it tells about only one part of the story.

Match the statements with the three answer choices below by writing the letter of each answer in the box in front of the statement it goes with.

**M—Main Idea      B—Too Broad      N—Too Narrow**

_____ ☐ 1. The fishing schooner *Charles Haskell* was haunted by the ghosts of the crew of the *Andrew Johnson,* a boat the *Haskell* rammed and sank.

_____ ☐ 2. The schooner *Charles Haskell* rammed and sank the *Andrew Johnson* during a storm on Georges Bank.

_____ ☐ 3. The *Charles Haskell* was a fishing schooner that was cursed with bad luck from the start.

_____ Score 15 points for a correct *M* answer

_____ Score 5 points for each correct *B* or *N* answer

_____ TOTAL SCORE: Finding the Main Idea

## B  RECALLING FACTS

How well do you remember the facts in the story you just read?
Put an x in the box in front of the correct answer to each of the
multiple choice questions below.

1. The home port of the *Charles Haskell* was
   - ___ ☐ a. Gloucester.
   - ___ ☐ b. Essex.
   - ___ ☐ c. Boston.

2. The man who commissioned the *Haskell*
   - ___ ☐ a. became its first captain.
   - ___ ☐ b. sank the *Andrew Johnson*.
   - ___ ☐ c. refused to accept the vessel.

3. When a storm arose on Georges Bank, the captains
   of the fishing schooners would
   - ___ ☐ a. anchor until the storm passed.
   - ___ ☐ b. try to sail for home as fast as they could.
   - ___ ☐ c. continue fishing.

4. Ghosts were first seen aboard the *Haskell*
   - ___ ☐ a. in Gloucester.
   - ___ ☐ b. just outside Gloucester.
   - ___ ☐ c. on Georges Bank.

5. The *Charles Haskell* eventually
   - ___ ☐ a. was sunk in Gloucester Harbor.
   - ___ ☐ b. sank on Georges Bank in a storm.
   - ___ ☐ c. rotted at its wharf.

Score 5 points for each correct answer

___ TOTAL SCORE: Recalling Facts

## C  MAKING INFERENCES

An inference is a judgment that is made or an idea that is
arrived at based on facts or on information that is given. You
make an inference when you understand something that is *not*
stated directly, but that is *implied,* or suggested by the facts that
are given.

Below are five statements that are judgments or ideas that
have been arrived at from the facts of the story. Write the letter
*C* in the box in front of each statement that is a correct inference. Write the letter *F* in front of each faulty inference.

**C—Correct Inference**     **F—Faulty Inference**

- ___ ☐ 1. It would have been very difficult for the *Haskell*
  to try to save the crew of the *Johnson*.

- ___ ☐ 2. Captain Curtis was an experienced sailor.

- ___ ☐ 3. Other fishermen held Captain Curtis responsible
  for the sinking of the *Andrew Johnson*.

- ___ ☐ 4. Few fishermen today risk fishing on Georges
  Bank.

- ___ ☐ 5. The *Andrew Johnson* was a poorly made boat.

Score 5 points for each correct answer

___ TOTAL SCORE: Making Inferences

## D  USING WORDS PRECISELY

Each of the numbered sentences below contains an underlined word or phrase from the story you have just read. Under the sentence are three definitions. One has the *same* meaning as the underlined word or phrase, one has *almost the same* meaning, and one has the *opposite* meaning. Match the definitions with the three answer choices by writing the letter that stands for each answer in the box in front of the definition it goes with.

**S—Same     A—Almost the Same     O—Opposite**

1. Dense fog can drop like a heavy curtain, <u>obscuring</u> everything beyond a few feet of one's eyes.

____  ☐ a. concealing

____  ☐ b. darkening

____  ☐ c. revealing

2. Sudden squalls and fierce gales have been known to <u>devastate</u> entire fishing fleets—sending some boats limping home and others plunging to the bottom of the sea.

____  ☐ a. damage

____  ☐ b. destroy

____  ☐ c. create

3. Now, sailors are nothing if not superstitious, so it was no surprise when the captain who had <u>commissioned</u> the *Haskell* refused to accept the vessel.

____  ☐ a. turned down

____  ☐ b. ordered to be made

____  ☐ c. hired

4. Within minutes the *Johnson* had sunk to the bottom, its crew leaping into the <u>roiling</u> waters.

____  ☐ a. calm

____  ☐ b. moving

____  ☐ c. disturbed

5. As the two men stood <u>transfixed</u>, six more ghostly figures silently climbed aboard the *Haskell* from the dark waters.

____  ☐ a. spellbound

____  ☐ b. unimpressed

____  ☐ c. still

____  Score 3 points for each correct *S* answer
____  Score 1 point for each correct *A* or *O* answer

____  TOTAL SCORE: Using Words Precisely

● *Enter the four total scores in the spaces below, and add them together to find your Critical Reading Score. Then record your Critical Reading Score on the graph on page 157.*

_____  Finding the Main Idea
_____  Recalling Facts
_____  Making Inferences
_____  Using Words Precisely

_____  CRITICAL READING SCORE: Unit 13

Encounters with ghosts are commonly thought of as being scary, but the people who claimed to have crossed paths with Harvey were mainly either amused or annoyed. Harvey spent most of his time puzzling and startling people in the building shown here.

# Harvey of Fort Sam Houston

Windows opening and doors slamming for no apparent reason. Footsteps crunching in empty rooms. Music drifting out of a ceiling. The carriage of a typewriter moving back and forth as if driven by some unseen hand. Some twenty years ago, at Service Club Number 2 at the U.S. Army Medical Training Center in Fort Sam Houston, Texas, such strange happenings were almost taken for granted. The people who worked in the club would just shrug and say, "Harvey's at it again."

The Service Club was a social center for enlisted soldiers and their families, and they welcomed all manner of guests. Harvey was, without a doubt, the most unusual. You see, Harvey was a ghost. How he (or "it") came by the name Harvey is a mystery.

Those who encountered Harvey did not jump to the conclusion that they were dealing with a ghost. They were more sensible than that. No, they began by investigating every possible normal explanation for the strange events that took place. Finally, a ghost seemed to be the only plausible explanation.

Harvey was not malicious, as some ghosts are, but he could make quite a nuisance of himself. When Phyllis Boyes was director of the service club, in 1967 and 1968, Harvey's habit of opening windows that had been locked for the night used to drive her crazy.

"In the first place," Ms. Boyes explained, "when a building is left open here . . . it means the Military Police call you whenever they discover it, no matter what time of night. You then have to return to the building to check it out and make sure there hasn't been a break-in. This, at some unpleasant hour like two o'clock in the morning, can be quite irritating. So closing up the place and securing it is very important. This is why I got so put out with the young men to whom I entrusted this job. They assured me that they had carefully locked up in each case, but as they would leave the building, they would look back and see a window open. This happened time and time again, and I insisted the men were being very careless. Finally, we set up a system where one fellow would close up the building and then two of us would go around checking on him. We would then leave, vowing that all the windows and doors were thoroughly locked. We might still, as like as not, find an upstairs window open when we looked back."

Army First Sergeant Louis Milligan confirmed Ms. Boyes's statement. On more than one occasion he locked all the windows in the building, only to find one or more open when he got outside and looked around.

Could the locks have been faulty? Were there broken sashes that allowed the windows to slip down by themselves? No, in both cases. Each window had been securely bolted, so the windows could not possibly have been opened unless someone had released the bolts.

Harvey made his presence known in other ways too. Sometimes he would walk around noisily, for his footsteps were frequently heard on the second floor of the Service Club. But whenever the upstairs rooms were searched, they were found to be empty. There didn't seem to be any way that a person could have left the building without being noticed, either, unless, of course, that "someone" happened to be a ghost!

On hearing the footsteps, one young soldier, who didn't believe in spirits, demanded that Harvey prove his existence. "Harvey, if you're up there, you got to make me know it," he demanded. A few minutes later, the young soldier heard the sound of a door slamming directly behind him. He whirled around, only to find the door wide open!

Then there was the musical incident. Sergeant Milligan described what happened when he and a worker were closing up the club one evening: "We had fastened up everything securely and were getting ready to leave. Then, just as we were in the lobby, we heard this beautiful music. It seemed to be coming out of the ceiling." Both men clearly heard the music, which they said sounded as though it was made by a flute. When Sergeant Milligan went upstairs to investigate the source of the music, the sound stopped. When he went back down the stairs, it started up again.

Was there some natural cause for the music? Sergeant Milligan was certain the building was empty. But might a radio have been left on in some office? The offices were checked, but all the radios were off. Could a trickster have been hiding somewhere in the building? The janitors, who were intimately familiar with all the nooks and crannies of the building, were asked to check every possible hiding place. No one was ever discovered.

Shortly after the music episode, a type-writer apparently went into action on its own. There were two men in the room at the time. Both had their backs to the typewriter when they suddenly heard the carriage slide across the machine so force-fully that the end-of-line bell rang. Neither soldier could have moved the carriage without the other's being aware of it.

Another witness to Harvey's antics claimed to have heard the characteristic sounds of a table tennis game being played. "It went 'ping, pong, pong,' " she said, "but no one else was in the room." Could Harvey have invited a fellow ghost in for a night of recreation?

Yet another person claimed to have heard Harvey clear his throat. That person was putting some food back into a refrigerator when she heard someone "har-rumph" right behind her. Although she reminded herself that ghosts do not have throats to clear, she could find no one else in the building.

Not all of Harvey's antics were confined to Service Club Number 2. Sergeant Milligan related a story about his electric saw, which disappeared from his home not far from the club. "I was doing some work at home one Saturday and decided to use the saw, but when I looked for it, I couldn't find it. . . . I searched for it all over the house, but it was not there. . . . When I got to my office here on Fort Sam Houston, my electric saw was under my desk. I don't know from that day to this how that saw got under my desk."

The sergeant was sure no one could have borrowed or stolen his saw. He was equally certain he was not the one who put it in his office. "Such a thing worries you," he said at the time. "It is frightening."

"Frightening" was not the word most people used in describing Harvey, how-ever. He never harmed anyone. Indeed, he seemed more playful than anything else.

At Fort Sam Houston, people learned to take his antics in stride.

Harvey eventually left. Why, no one seems to know. Nothing has been heard from him in more than fifteen years, and there are no indications that he will ever return. Service Club Number 2, now carrying the fashionable title of Hacienda Recreation Center, is once again a ghost-free gathering place.

Well then, who was Harvey, and what was he doing at the club? The most commonly accepted theory is that Harvey was the ghost of a young man who committed suicide in the club. But only the fact of the young man's violent death—not the *why* of it—is on record.

Whoever Harvey was and why ever he decided to hang around Service Club Number 2, he provided some entertaining times for the folks at Fort Sam Houston. ■

*If you have been timed while reading this selection, enter your reading time below. Then turn to the Words per Minute table on page 155 and look up your reading speed (words per minute). Enter your reading speed on the graph on page 156.*

READING TIME: Unit 14

_____ : _____

*Minutes*          *Seconds*

# How well did you read?

- *Answer the four types of questions that follow. The directions for each type of question tell you how to mark your answers.*

- *When you have finished all four exercises, check your work by using the answer key on page 151. For each right answer, put a check mark (✔) on the line beside the box. For each wrong answer, write the correct answer on the line.*

- *For scoring each exercise, follow the directions below the questions.*

## A FINDING THE MAIN IDEA

Look at the three statements below. One expresses the main idea of the story you just read. A good main idea statement answers two questions: it tells *who* or *what* is the subject of the story, and it answers the understood question *does what?* or *is what?* Another statement is *too broad*, it is vague and doesn't tell much about the topic of the story. The third statement is *too narrow*, it tells about only one part of the story.

Match the statements with the three answer choices below by writing the letter of each answer in the box in front of the statement it goes with.

**M—Main Idea**   **B—Too Broad**   **N—Too Narrow**

_____ ☐ 1. Unexplained occurrences at Fort Sam Houston in Texas kept people there baffled for two years.

_____ ☐ 2. Though Harvey startled people and caused some problems, he never harmed anyone.

_____ ☐ 3. A playful ghost named Harvey baffled and entertained people at Service Club Number 2 at Fort Sam Houston in the late 1960s.

_____ Score 15 points for a correct *M* answer

_____ Score 5 points for each correct *B* or *N* answer

_____ TOTAL SCORE: Finding the Main Idea

## B  RECALLING FACTS

How well do you remember the facts in the story you just read? Put an *x* in the box in front of the correct answer to each of the multiple choice questions below.

1. Service Club Number 2 was a
   - ☐ a. sports club.
   - ☐ b. recreation center.
   - ☐ c. dining hall.

2. Phyllis Boyes's main problem with Harvey was that he
   - ☐ a. played loud music at all hours.
   - ☐ b. frightened people away from the club.
   - ☐ c. kept opening the windows of the club.

3. One witness claimed to hear Harvey playing
   - ☐ a. table tennis.
   - ☐ b. pool.
   - ☐ c. basketball.

4. The object that Sergeant Milligan said was missing from his home and then turned up in his office was
   - ☐ a. an ax.
   - ☐ b. a hammer.
   - ☐ c. a saw.

5. The most commonly accepted explanation for Harvey is that he was the ghost of
   - ☐ a. a soldier who was killed in a battle at the fort in the Civil War.
   - ☐ b. a man who killed himself in the club.
   - ☐ c. the first commander of Fort Sam Houston.

Score 5 points for each correct answer

_____ TOTAL SCORE: Recalling Facts

## C  MAKING INFERENCES

An inference is a judgment that is made or an idea that is arrived at based on facts or on information that is given. You make an inference when you understand something that is *not* stated directly, but that is *implied*, or suggested by the facts that are given.

Below are five statements that are judgments or ideas that have been arrived at from the facts of the story. Write the letter C in the box in front of each statement that is a correct inference. Write the letter F in front of each faulty inference.

**C—Correct Inference**     **F—Faulty Inference**

1. Phyllis Boyes was a harsh and unreasonable person to work for.

2. Since Harvey left, no music has been played in Service Club Number 2.

3. Some people enjoyed having Harvey around the club.

4. Harvey played each trick only once.

5. Phyllis Boyes was annoyed at Harvey's presence.

Score 5 points for each correct answer

_____ TOTAL SCORE: Making Inferences

## D USING WORDS PRECISELY

Each of the numbered sentences below contains an underlined word or phrase from the story you have just read. Under the sentence are three definitions. One has the *same* meaning as the underlined word or phrase, one has *almost the same* meaning, and one has the *opposite* meaning. Match the definitions with the three answer choices by writing the letter that stands for each answer in the box in front of the definition it goes with.

**S—Same      A—Almost the Same      O—Opposite**

1. Finally, a ghost seemed to be the only <u>plausible</u> answer.

____  ☐ a. improbable

____  ☐ b. logical

____  ☐ c. likely

2. Harvey was not <u>malicious</u>, as some ghosts are, but he could make quite a nuisance of himself.

____  ☐ a. mischievous

____  ☐ b. mean

____  ☐ c. friendly

3. So closing up the place and <u>securing</u> it is very important.

____  ☐ a. locking

____  ☐ b. fastening

____  ☐ c. freeing

4. The janitors, who were <u>intimately</u> familiar with all the nooks and crannies of the building, were asked to check every possible hiding place.

____  ☐ a. closely

____  ☐ b. thoroughly

____  ☐ c. slightly

5. Nothing has been heard from him in more than fifteen years, and there are no <u>indications</u> that he will ever return.

____  ☐ a. signs

____  ☐ b. lack of evidence

____  ☐ c. hints

____  Score 3 points for each correct *S* answer
____  Score 1 point for each correct *A* or *O* answer

____  TOTAL SCORE: Using Words Precisely

● *Enter the four total scores in the spaces below, and add them together to find your Critical Reading Score. Then record your Critical Reading Score on the graph on page 157.*

| | |
|---|---|
| _____ | Finding the Main Idea |
| _____ | Recalling Facts |
| _____ | Making Inferences |
| _____ | Using Words Precisely |
| _____ | CRITICAL READING SCORE: Unit 14 |

# GROUP THREE

# The Return of Nelly Butler

One day late in January, in the year 1800, Captain Paul Blaisdel saw a most unusual sight. He was walking through a field when an "unreal-looking" figure of a woman appeared in the distance. Her clothes, he later said, were "as white as possible," and she seemed to float over the ground. The apparition moved quickly toward him, but before Blaisdel could say a word, it vanished into thin air.

Ghosts were not common in the town of Machiasport, Maine. Until then, there was no record of anyone in the town ever having seen one. But Paul Blaisdel's ghostly encounter was only the beginning of what would prove to be a unique supernatural experience for scores of people in that seacoast town.

Paul Blaisdel was the first to see the apparition, but a few months earlier, on August 9, 1799, the spirit had made its presence known at the home of Paul's father, Abner Blaisdel. A voice, seeming to come out of nowhere, announced to the family that its ghostly figure would soon appear in the village. The Blaisdels were dumbfounded. They had no idea who the voice belonged to. But they did know enough to keep the story to themselves, since the hard-working, practical people of Machiasport would certainly have laughed in their faces.

As months went by and the voice remained silent, the Blaisdels forgot about the announcement. On January 2, 1800, however, the voice spoke again. That time it revealed its owner. "I am Captain George Butler's deceased wife, Nelly," it said. "My father is David Hooper."

The Blaisdels knew both these men well. In fact, they had also known Nelly Butler before her death. "Send two messengers to fetch my father," the voice ordered in a tone that left no room for argument. The Blaisdels did as they were told.

David Hooper was an old man, and six miles was a long trip for what he considered "plumb foolishness," but when he got to the Blaisdel house and heard the voice, he was convinced that it was indeed his daughter speaking. Later he wrote that she gave "such clear and irresistible tokens of her being the spirit of my own daughter as gave me no less satisfaction than admiration and delight."

Later that month, "the spectre," as the townsfolk called the apparition, appeared to Paul Blaisdel in the field. Apparently, though, she was not happy with his reaction. The day after the encounter, Nelly appeared at the Blaisdel home to chide Paul for being rude to an old friend and neighbor.

After that visit, Nelly stayed away for several weeks. She returned again in March for a chat. She insisted that all four Blaisdels gather in the cellar, where she talked to them for two hours. "Though my body is consumed and turned to dust," she said, "my soul is as much alive as before I left the body."

In May she returned six nights in a row. By that time the apparition was the talk of the town, and the Blaisdels were being bombarded with visitors. The curious were taken to the cellar, which was the spectre's favorite spot. According to witnesses, the spectre usually appeared dressed in shining white, and the brightness of her body lit the area around her. All agreed that she looked like the person she said she was—the deceased Nelly Butler.

One witness, Mary Gordon, who visited the Blaisdels' cellar as part of a group, described her experience with the spectre this way: "At first the apparition was a mere mass of light. Then it grew into personal form, about as tall as myself. We stood in two ranks, about four or five feet apart. Between these ranks she slowly passed and repassed, so that any of us could have handled her. When she passed by me, her nearness was that of contact, so that if there had been a substance, I should have certainly felt it. The glow of the apparition had a constant tremulous

August 13–14, I was there ag...
tion of the ghost, with several other persons in ...
cerning several events known only to her and them in her life
time. To all their questions she gave satisfactory answers.
Once while she was speaking, I saw a bright shining appearance in that part of the space from whence the voice proceeded.
Her conversation and exhortation continued four hours.—
One of the company observed to her that we were an hardened
people. "Yes," she answered, "But the Lord will call in
his elect in his own time." I went to Capt. M's with the
...my, but did not then see her at all.

ABIGAIL ABBOT.

...IMONY XII.

...f Miss Dorcas Abbot.
...d ear witness, to all that is declared
...last testimony.
...tler's hand go through the apparition.

DORCAS ABBOT.

...TIMONY XIII.

...of Mr. Frederic Housoff.
...witness of all the facts declared in th...
...attest particularly that I plainly sa...
...nd on the apparition, and saw his ha...
...g with the light of it.

FREDERIC HOUSOFF

...ESTIMONY XIV.

Testimony of Mr. Joseph Blaisdel.
I was present when the important transaction took plac...
the night of August 9, 1800, and saw Mr. Butler's hand
through the body of the apparition, while he uttered the w...
"Lord Jesus." He afterwards informed me and o...
that while his hand passed through the breast of the Sp...
he felt nothing.

JOSEPH BLAISD...

TESTIMONY XV.

Testimony of Capt. Paul Blaisdel.
I have seen and discoursed with the apparition severa...
In the latter part of January, 1800, I saw her in the ...
first at a considerable distance from me; then she cam...
and I particularly observed that she never touched the ...
Her raiment appeared as white as possible. The next ...
she reproved me in the bearing of several persons, ...

motion. At last the personal form became shapeless—expanded every way, and then vanished in a moment."

Despite the written testimony of dozens of witnesses, many people were skeptical of the apparition. One doubter was Abraham Cummings, a minister and a well-educated man. But Cummings changed his mind when he saw the spectre for himself. Crossing an open field in front of his house, the minister saw a group of white rocks on a small hill about two hundred feet in front of him. As he walked toward them, one of the rocks rose off the ground and began taking the shape of a globe of rosy light. Suddenly the light moved near to him, and took on the shape of a very tiny woman. She grew to normal size, and Cummings said she looked "glorious," with rays of light shining from her head like a halo reaching to the ground.

That experience changed the minister's life. He became a convert, and set out to record every appearance the spectre made. He later published an account of the events, which included the testimony of every witness he could contact. Several copies of Abraham Cummings's pamphlet are still in existence (one of them can be found in the Brown University library, in Rhode Island), but Cummings was, unfortunately, a boring and often confusing writer.

*The many people who saw and talked with the ghost of Nelly Butler were so sure the apparition was real that they gave sworn testimonies of their experiences with her. The testimonies were recorded in a pamphlet describing the events surrounding the ghost's stay in Machiasport, Maine. The residents of Machiasport were steady, no-nonsense folks, so the fact that they were convinced of the genuineness of the ghost is good enough reason to seriously consider the matter.*

Though Cummings grew to believe in the existence of the spectre, there were many who suspected the Blaisdels of fraud. One reason for their suspicion was the fact that the spectre ordered her former husband, Captain George Butler, to marry Abner Blaisdel's daughter Lydia. Abner was against the marriage, and so was Lydia. Although she was attracted to George, she refused to "marry a man who has been scared into proposing by a ghost."

However, when Captain Butler insisted that he wanted to marry Lydia for himself, and not because his dead wife ordered him to, Lydia changed her mind. Then the gossiping began in earnest. Folks said that Lydia had thought up the hoax to get herself a husband.

The spectre tried to prove Lydia's innocence. Once she appeared to a large gathering at which Lydia was present. She ordered Lydia to go to another room, where she was watched by two women. While Lydia was gone, Nelly continued to carry on in the cellar, proving that Lydia had no part in her performance. Another time the spectre marched next to Lydia in a funeral procession, so that everyone could see the two of them together.

Nonetheless, the gossip and suspicions continued. Finally, unable to bear up against the accusations, Lydia broke her engagement and made plans to visit relatives who lived farther down the coast. But before she could sail away, the spectre intervened and convinced her that she could not escape the gossip. Lydia and George were married shortly afterward.

By that time, Nelly had been appearing in Machiasport for over a year. She seemed to enjoy showing off her powers, which included predicting the future. She told the Blaisdels of a law suit that they would be involved in, and of how it would come out. She also predicted some bad news. Shortly after Lydia and George were married, the spectre appeared to George. "Be kind to Lydia," she said, "for she will not be with you long. She will have one child and die within the year." Ten months after the wedding, Lydia gave birth and died the next day.

Captain Butler never doubted that the spectre was the spirit of his dead wife. Nelly visited him several times and recalled conversations that they'd had during their life together—conversations that only she could have known about. Once she appeared before him carrying a very small child, a reminder, he thought, of the fact that she too had died in childbirth. Speaking of the apparition of the baby, Butler later said, "I reached out my left hand to take hold of it. I saw my hand in the middle of it, but could feel nothing." Four witnesses confirmed Butler's claim.

After Lydia's death, the spectre disappeared from Machiasport, never to return. Although more than a hundred observers claimed to have seen or heard her, one important question remained unanswered: Why had she come in the first place?

Whatever the reason, Nelly Butler holds a special place in United States history. Thanks to Abraham Cummings, she was the first ghost to be written about in an account featuring sworn testimonies. And she was witnessed by more people than any other ghost, before or since. ■

*If you have been timed while reading this selection, enter your reading time below. Then turn to the Words per Minute table on page 155 and look up your reading speed (words per minute). Enter your reading speed on the graph on page 156.*

READING TIME: Unit 15

_____ : _____
*Minutes*      *Seconds*

# How well did you read?

- *Answer the four types of questions that follow. The directions for each type of question tell you how to mark your answers.*

- *When you have finished all four exercises, check your work by using the answer key on page 152. For each right answer, put a check mark (✔) on the line beside the box. For each wrong answer, write the correct answer on the line.*

- *For scoring each exercise, follow the directions below the questions.*

## A FINDING THE MAIN IDEA

Look at the three statements below. One expresses the main idea of the story you just read. A good main idea statement answers two questions: it tells *who* or *what* is the subject of the story, and it answers the understood question *does what?* or *is what?* Another statement is *too broad*, it is vague and doesn't tell much about the topic of the story. The third statement is *too narrow*, it tells about only one part of the story.

Match the statements with the three answer choices below by writing the letter of each answer in the box in front of the statement it goes with.

**M—Main Idea    B—Too Broad    N—Too Narrow**

_____ ☐ 1. The ghost of Nelly Butler appeared in Machiasport, Maine, many times around 1800, becoming the most widely witnessed ghost in history.

_____ ☐ 2. Nelly Butler's ghost appeared in Machiasport, Maine.

_____ ☐ 3. A ghost in a small New England town captured the attention of the townspeople for more than a year in the early nineteenth century.

_____ Score 15 points for a correct *M* answer

_____ Score 5 points for each correct *B* or *N* answer

_____ TOTAL SCORE: Finding the Main Idea

## B RECALLING FACTS

How well do you remember the facts in the story you just read? Put an *x* in the box in front of the correct answer to each of the multiple choice questions below.

1. The first person the ghost of Nelly Butler appeared to was
   ___ □ a. Paul Blaisdel.
   ___ □ b. George Butler.
   ___ □ c. Abner Blaisdel.

2. Nelly's favorite place to meet with people was in a
   ___ □ a. field.
   ___ □ b. cemetery.
   ___ □ c. cellar.

3. The main thing people noticed about the ghost of Nelly Butler was
   ___ □ a. the softness of her voice.
   ___ □ b. brightness and light.
   ___ □ c. her sense of humor.

4. Lydia Blaisdel was going to leave Machiasport because she
   ___ □ a. didn't want to marry George Butler.
   ___ □ b. was afraid of the ghost of Nelly Butler.
   ___ □ c. couldn't stand the unkind gossip people were spreading about her.

5. The ghost of Nelly Butler left Machiasport when
   ___ □ a. Lydia Blaisdel died.
   ___ □ b. George Butler remarried.
   ___ □ c. Abraham Cummings had finished his book.

Score 5 points for each correct answer

___ TOTAL SCORE: Recalling Facts

## C MAKING INFERENCES

An inference is a judgment that is made or an idea that is arrived at based on facts or on information that is given. You make an inference when you understand something that is *not* stated directly, but that is *implied*, or suggested by the facts that are given.

Below are five statements that are judgments or ideas that have been arrived at from the facts of the story. Write the letter *C* in the box in front of each statement that is a correct inference. Write the letter *F* in front of each faulty inference.

**C—Correct Inference    F—Faulty Inference**

___ □ 1. Many people in Machiasport were frightened of the ghost of Nelly Butler.

___ □ 2. Lydia's baby died.

___ □ 3. David Hooper was happy to see the ghost of his daughter.

___ □ 4. Nelly Butler liked Lydia Blaisdel.

___ □ 5. George Butler never married again after Lydia's death.

Score 5 points for each correct answer

___ TOTAL SCORE: Making Inferences

## D USING WORDS PRECISELY

Each of the numbered sentences below contains an underlined word or phrase from the story you have just read. Under the sentence are three definitions. One has the *same* meaning as the underlined word or phrase, one has *almost the same* meaning, and one has the *opposite* meaning. Match the definitions with the three answer choices by writing the letter that stands for each answer in the box in front of the definition it goes with.

**S—Same        A—Almost the Same        O—Opposite**

1. "Send two messengers to <u>fetch</u> my father," the voice ordered in a tone that left no room for argument.

____  ☐ a. get

____  ☐ b. locate

____  ☐ c. leave

2. The day after the encounter, Nelly appeared at the Blaisdel home to <u>chide</u> Paul for being rude to an old friend and neighbor.

____  ☐ a. attack

____  ☐ b. praise

____  ☐ c. scold

3. Despite the written testimony of dozens of witnesses, many people were <u>skeptical</u> of the apparition.

____  ☐ a. sure

____  ☐ b. doubtful

____  ☐ c. uncertain

4. He later published an <u>account</u> of the events, which included the testimony of every witness he could contact.

____  ☐ a. statement

____  ☐ b. opinion

____  ☐ c. description

5. But before she could sail away, the spectre <u>intervened</u> and convinced her that she could not escape the gossip.

____  ☐ a. stepped in

____  ☐ b. withdrew

____  ☐ c. interfered

____ Score 3 points for each correct *S* answer

____ Score 1 point for each correct *A* or *O* answer

____ TOTAL SCORE: Using Words Precisely

● *Enter the four total scores in the spaces below, and add them together to find your Critical Reading Score. Then record your Critical Reading Score on the graph on page 157.*

| | |
|---|---|
| _____ | Finding the Main Idea |
| _____ | Recalling Facts |
| _____ | Making Inferences |
| _____ | Using Words Precisely |
| _____ | CRITICAL READING SCORE: Unit 15 |

In Beverly Hills, you might expect reports of a ghost to be part of a publicity stunt. After all, most of the residents of that exclusive California suburb are involved in movies and television. But if actress Elke Sommer was looking for attention, she sure went to an unusual extreme. The ghost that was supposedly disturbing her home life was linked with a fire that severely damaged her house. The incident persuaded Elke that ghosts—or at least that particular ghost—did not make good housemates.

# A Beverly Hills Ghost

The residents of Beverly Hills, California, include some of the most famous faces in the world—movie stars, sports figures, TV personalities. At least one of the residents of that well-known city has had an uninvited and decidedly unwelcome housemate—one that caused a lot of confusion and not a little consternation.

Actress Elke Sommer and her husband, reporter Joe Hyams, met the intruder shortly after moving into their new house in July of 1964. A guest of theirs, a journalist named Edith Dohlfield, was having tea by the pool when she noticed a man suddenly appear, walk quickly around the pool, and then disappear. She later described the man as middle-aged, husky, and broad-shouldered, with a "potato nose." He was wearing dark slacks with a white shirt and a tie. When Edith asked who the man was, Elke and Joe said they had no idea.

A similar experience was reported about two weeks later. A person cleaning the pool said he saw an older, heavy-set man with graying hair walking quickly toward the dining room. The stranger was dressed in dark trousers and a white shirt with a tie. Since the pool cleaner had been told that the owners were away and the house would be empty, he decided to investigate. When he followed the man into the house, however, he found no trace of anyone.

Elke Sommer's mother, who was visiting at the house, was the third person to see the strange man. He woke her in the middle of the night. Just as she was about to scream, he vanished into thin air.

Up to that point, neither Elke Sommer nor Joe Hyams had noticed anything out of the ordinary in their new house. Then they began hearing strange noises, such as the sound of chairs scraping across the floor in the dining room at night. Whenever they checked the room, however, everything was in its proper place.

In August, when Elke was making a film in Yugoslavia and Joe was staying alone in the house, he witnessed a series of unexplainable events. Each morning he found a bedroom window on the first floor wide open, even though he always locked the window at night. At times he heard the front door open and shut when no one else was in the house. Although he was growing more and more concerned about the strange things that were happening, Hyams was sure there was a logical explanation for everything. A journalist for fifteen years, he was a believer in facts.

Determined to get to the bottom of the matter, he bought three small radio transmitters and set them up in different places: at the end of the driveway, at the front door, and in the dining room. He wired three tape recorders to the transmitters and hooked them up, in turn, to three FM radios, which he placed upstairs in his bedroom. When the equipment was turned on, any sounds made near the transmitters would be heard in the bedroom and would also be recorded. Using chalk, Joe then marked the placement of each dining room chair so that he could tell if any of the chairs had been moved.

His efforts were soon rewarded. On the first night of his surveillance, he heard the same scraping sounds he had heard so often before. He stole quietly down the stairs and into the dining room, only to find that no one was there and the chairs were all in their proper places. As soon as he went back upstairs, though, the noises resumed.

In September John Sherlock, a writer friend whom Joe Hyams described as having a "cool, careful mind," stayed in the house while Elke and Joe were away. He heard the same noises and noticed the same strange and inexplicable opening of the downstairs window. When he was preparing to go to bed one evening, he suddenly had the eerie sensation that someone was watching him. He turned to see a man staring at him from the doorway—a man wearing dark trousers, a white shirt, and a dark tie. Sherlock was so frightened that he immediately moved into a motel. "I never had such a feeling of menace," he later told Hyams.

The same strange events persisted, and new ones were added. A detective who had been hired to watch the house reported that once all the lights in the house were turned on at the same time; there was no one home. Also, Elke and Joe's two dogs started acting restless and standing at the entrance to the dining room, barking at nothing. The strange noises continued.

Still sure that there had to be a logical explanation, Hyams hired a team of termite inspectors to look for hidden entrances to the house. None were found. An architect hired to search for hidden rooms in the house also found nothing.

Finally, at Joe Hyams's request, professional ghost hunters became involved in the case. They began by questioning the four witnesses who had reported seeing the strange man. Each was asked to describe the man, including what he looked like, what he had been doing when they saw him, and what kind of impression he gave. The witnesses were asked to be as specific as possible. One of the investigative team, who remained in New York, then analyzed the reports in an attempt to come up with a composite description of the man.

The next step was to bring a number of strangers into the house, one at a time, to see if they could sense a presence. Some of the people selected said that they had never seen a ghost before. Others were "sensitives"—people who claim to be able to communicate with spirits. Although no one had been told any details about the apparition in Elke and Joe's house, four of the people said that they sensed a presence in the dining room, and three described a man who sounded much like the one seen by the four witnesses. Some of the details of the man's appearance reminded Joe Hyams of a doctor he had worked with who had recently died. He also sounded somewhat like Elke Sommer's father, who was dead.

The sensitives provided further impressions. One claimed to have seen a girl near the pool, and gave a description that sounded much like a girl whom Elke Sommer had known in Europe and who had died recently. Another sensitive predicted that there would be a fire in the house, perhaps within six months, and that it would be raining at the time. She also predicted that Elke and Joe would move out of the house within two years.

The conclusion drawn by the ghost hunters was somewhat disappointing. It was possible, but only possible, they said, that the house was haunted. Without more evidence, they were unwilling to make a more definite statement.

By that time, however, Elke and Joe had reached their own conclusion. Thorough searches of the house by termite inspectors, private detectives, and electronics experts had convinced them that no human being or animal was causing the problems. A geologist had reported that the land was not shifting. A construction expert had stated that the house was solid. After eliminating every logical explanation, Joe Hyams stated, "Even I am reluctantly convinced that we have at least one ghost in the house. But," he added, "we don't intend to move out. I would not let a living man frighten me out of my house, and I certainly don't intend to let a dead one do it."

It wasn't long before he changed his mind. Early in the morning, on March 13, 1967, during a rare California rainstorm, Elke and Joe were awakened by loud pounding on their bedroom door. When they opened the door, they were engulfed by smoke. The house was on fire. Luckily, they were able to crawl out a window to safety, and fire fighters arrived in time to put out the blaze.

Although an investigation into the fire was unable to pinpoint a cause, it was found that the fire had started in the dining room. Enough was enough, Elke and Joe decided. Just as the sensitive had predicted, they moved to a new house—one that contained no uninvited guests. ∎

*If you have been timed while reading this selection, enter your reading time below. Then turn to the Words per Minute table on page 155 and look up your reading speed (words per minute). Enter your reading speed on the graph on page 156.*

READING TIME: Unit 16

———————— : ————————
*Minutes*            *Seconds*

# How well did you read?

- *Answer the four types of questions that follow. The directions for each type of question tell you how to mark your answers.*

- *When you have finished all four exercises, check your work by using the answer key on page 152. For each right answer, put a check mark (✔) on the line beside the box. For each wrong answer, write the correct answer on the line.*

- *For scoring each exercise, follow the directions below the questions.*

## A  FINDING THE MAIN IDEA

Look at the three statements below. One expresses the main idea of the story you just read. A good main idea statement answers two questions: it tells *who* or *what* is the subject of the story, and it answers the understood question *does what?* or *is what?* Another statement is *too broad*, it is vague and doesn't tell much about the topic of the story. The third statement is *too narrow*, it tells about only one part of the story.

Match the statements with the three answer choices below by writing the letter of each answer in the box in front of the statement it goes with.

**M—Main Idea**    **B—Too Broad**    **N—Too Narrow**

____ ☐ 1. Elke Sommer and Joe Hyams were forced to leave their house by an intruder that they finally decided had to be a ghost.

____ ☐ 2. Strange occurrences in Elke Sommer and Joe Hyams's house frightened and perplexed those who stayed in the house.

____ ☐ 3. In and just outside Elke Sommer and Joe Hyams's house, a number of people saw a strange man appear and then vanish.

____ Score 15 points for a correct *M* answer

____ Score 5 points for each correct *B* or *N* answer

____ TOTAL SCORE: Finding the Main Idea

## B RECALLING FACTS

How well do you remember the facts in the story you just read? Put an *x* in the box in front of the correct answer to each of the multiple choice questions below.

1. Joe Hyams was a
   - ___ ☐ a. movie director.
   - ___ ☐ b. journalist.
   - ___ ☐ c. record producer.

2. The strange man was first seen
   - ___ ☐ a. near the pool.
   - ___ ☐ b. entering the dining room.
   - ___ ☐ c. near the bedroom door.

3. The ghost hunters concluded that
   - ___ ☐ a. the house was definitely haunted.
   - ___ ☐ b. there was no ghost in the house.
   - ___ ☐ c. it was possible that the house was haunted.

4. The fire in the house
   - ___ ☐ a. originated in the bedroom.
   - ___ ☐ b. took place during a rainstorm.
   - ___ ☐ c. destroyed most of the house.

5. Elke and Joe became convinced that
   - ___ ☐ a. there was a ghost in the house.
   - ___ ☐ b. someone was playing an unpleasant hoax on them.
   - ___ ☐ c. someone who didn't like them was trying to frighten them.

Score 5 points for each correct answer

___ TOTAL SCORE: Recalling Facts

## C MAKING INFERENCES

An inference is a judgment that is made or an idea that is arrived at based on facts or on information that is given. You make an inference when you understand something that is *not* stated directly, but that is *implied,* or suggested by the facts that are given.

Below are five statements that are judgments or ideas that have been arrived at from the facts of the story. Write the letter *C* in the box in front of each statement that is a correct inference. Write the letter *F* in front of each faulty inference.

**C—Correct Inference     F—Faulty Inference**

- ___ ☐ 1. No one ever found out who the strange man was.
- ___ ☐ 2. The strange man never spoke.
- ___ ☐ 3. The ghost hunters were frauds.
- ___ ☐ 4. Neither Elke nor Joe ever became frightened of the presence in their house.
- ___ ☐ 5. No one has lived in the house since Elke and Joe moved out.

Score 5 points for each correct answer

___ TOTAL SCORE: Making Inferences

## D USING WORDS PRECISELY

Each of the numbered sentences below contains an underlined word or phrase from the story you have just read. Under the sentence are three definitions. One has the *same* meaning as the underlined word or phrase, one has *almost the same* meaning, and one has the *opposite* meaning. Match the definitions with the three answer choices by writing the letter that stands for each answer in the box in front of the definition it goes with.

**S—Same    A—Almost the Same    O—Opposite**

1. At least one of the residents of that well-known city has had an uninvited and decidedly unwelcome housemate—one that caused a lot of confusion and not a little <u>consternation</u>.

____ ☐ a. comfort

____ ☐ b. alarm

____ ☐ c. terror

2. On the first night of his <u>surveillance</u>, he heard the same scraping sounds he had heard so often before.

____ ☐ a. close watch

____ ☐ b. ignoring

____ ☐ c. supervision

3. He <u>stole</u> quietly down the stairs and into the dining room, only to find that no one was there and the chairs were all in their proper places.

____ ☐ a. slinked

____ ☐ b. moved boldly

____ ☐ c. sneaked

4. He heard the same noises and noticed the same strange and <u>inexplicable</u> opening of the downstairs window.

____ ☐ a. unexplainable

____ ☐ b. confusing

____ ☐ c. understandable

5. "I never had such a feeling of <u>menace</u>," he later told Hyams.

____ ☐ a. evil

____ ☐ b. comfort

____ ☐ c. threat

____ Score 3 points for each correct *S* answer

____ Score 1 point for each correct *A* or *O* answer

____ **TOTAL SCORE:** Using Words Precisely

● *Enter the four total scores in the spaces below, and add them together to find your Critical Reading Score. Then record your Critical Reading Score on the graph on page 157.*

_____ Finding the Main Idea
_____ Recalling Facts
_____ Making Inferences
_____ Using Words Precisely
_____ **CRITICAL READING SCORE: Unit 16**

*Just about everyone in the German Navy during World War I knew about the submarine called the U-65. It was part of a fleet of U-boats that Germany proudly regarded as its strongest weapon in the war. The U-65 stood out among all the others. In the eyes of most sailors, it was jinxed. No one wanted to serve aboard it. From beginning to mysterious end, the U-65 was visited by catastrophe.*

# The Haunted U-Boat

It was 1916, the midpoint of World War I, and the tide was beginning to turn against the Germans. Their soldiers were dug into positions in France, unable to advance. A British blockade of German harbors kept German supply ships from moving in and out of their own ports. In the United States, preparations to enter the war were underway; the country did so a year later. So it was no surprise when the Germans began building ships in the city of Bruges, Belgium, which they had occupied. The ships were *unterseeboots*, or U-boats, as German submarines were commonly called, and twenty-four of them were being built.

Construction went smoothly on the first twenty-three boats, but the twenty-fourth, designated the U-65, was another story. Several workers were killed while building it. Then on launching day, in October of 1916, as the U-65 was finally eased into the water, one of its officers fell overboard to his death.

That was far from the end of the submarine's troubles. U-65 put out to sea for trials, and on its first dive was stuck underwater, unable to resurface, for more than twelve hours. Sailors being a superstitious lot by nature, the crew was terrified at that near catastrophe. U-65 proceeded back to port, where it was

examined thoroughly. No reason for the malfunction could be found.

The day after the examination, a torpedo exploded on deck during a loading exercise, killing an officer and five crewmen. That incident lead to the first sighting of a ghost on board the U-65—the ghost of the officer killed in the torpedo explosion.

By that time, the story of the unlucky U-65 had made its way through the entire U-boat fleet. Sailors were convinced that the U-65 was a Jonah—a jinxed boat—and that it was haunted. More than one crewman reported seeing the ghost of the dead officer. "We saw him come aboard and walk slowly to the bow," one sailor insisted. "He stood there, staring at us, with his arms folded across his chest."

Stories of that sort can quickly demoralize the crew of any warship. That was something the German high command could not afford to let happen to the U-65. The enormously successful U-boats were Germany's chief weapon in the war. The country needed every one it could build.

Doing his part to restore morale, the captain of the U-65 mustered his crew on the afterdeck. He spoke of Germany's need for U-boats. He acknowledged the great strain everyone was under. Then he broached the subject of the ghost. "I'm

sure it's just imagination," he said. "The accident was a sad experience for all of us. Just try to put it out of your minds."

Shortly after the captain's talk, the U-65 put out to sea on its first war patrol. That is when the ghost materialized on board for the second time. Even the captain was a witness. When the patrol ended, the U-65 headed back to Bruges, where it was to undergo normal maintenance before its next cruise against the enemy.

Back in port, another tragic incident occurred. Allied bombers struck Bruges in a lightning-fast raid, killing, among hundreds of others, the captain of the U-65. As might be expected, the talk of its being a Jonah revived.

This time Admiral Schroeder, head of the U-boat command, took matters into his own hands. After denouncing all talk of jinxed boats and ghosts as "superstitious nonsense," the admiral spent a night on board the U-65. In the morning he informed the crew that he had spent a restful night, undisturbed by any ghost. Still, to further placate the crew, he ordered that a clergyman perform an exorcism—a religious ceremony in which evil spirits are driven away—on board the U-65.

Admiral Schroeder's next step was to pick a new captain for the boat. He purposely chose a strict disciplinarian—Lieutenant Commander Gustav Schelle. The new captain immediately warned his crew that anyone even mentioning ghosts would be dealt with severely.

For nearly a year, through many war patrols, the U-65 performed admirably under Captain Schelle. There were no strange occurrences, and there was no evidence of a ghost. In fact, all went smoothly until May 1918, when the ghost returned, this time exhibiting a vindictive streak.

The first to feel its vengeance was Master Gunner Erich Eberhardt. A veteran of U-boats, not given to emotional outbursts of any kind, Gunner Eberhardt one day made a mad, panic-stricken dash into the control room. He was so wild that he had to be pinioned by the boat's guards. He kept babbling, "I've seen the ghost—an officer standing near the bow torpedo tubes. He brushed past me and disappeared!"

It took several crewmen to subdue the normally imperturbable gunner. Eberhardt was locked in the boat's tiny brig. When he was released hours later, having apparently recovered, he suddenly snatched a knife from a guard and killed himself on the spot.

Shortly after that incident, the U-65 surfaced to recharge its batteries. That was when Chief Petty Officer Richard Meyer, a close friend of the captain's, was swept over the side. His body was never recovered.

Officer Meyer's death spelled the end of the U-65's fighting efficiency. For the remainder of the patrol, the crew spent all its time trying to avoid, rather than engage, the enemy. Nevertheless, the boat was eventually hit by enemy shell fire and forced to limp back to Bruges for repairs.

As soon as the U-65 had tied up, an enraged Admiral Schroeder stormed on board. Wasting no time on explanations, he immediately relieved Captain Schelle of his command and had the entire crew transferred to other boats in the fleet. When the U-65 put out to sea again, in June 1918, it had a new captain and all new officers and crew.

The manner in which the U-65 met its end is quite as mystifying as the ghostly incidents that plagued it from the start. An American boat discovered the ill-starred U-boat lying on its side at sea on the morning of July 10, 1918. The American boat stood off for hours, its captain suspicious that the U-65 was a decoy, ready to explode should some unsuspecting enemy vessel close in to investigate. Finally, after hours of studying the U-boat that wallowed gently in the North Atlantic swells, the American captain gave his order: "Sink her. Ready all forward torpedo tubes!"

No sooner had he given that order than the U-65 was racked from within by a series of furious explosions. It broke into pieces and slipped to its watery grave. The American captain later reported that moments before the explosions he saw someone standing near the bow of the U-boat. It was, he said, the figure of a German naval officer dressed in a great-coat, his arms folded across his chest.

"The War to End All Wars," as World War I was called, ended on November 11, 1918, with the Allies as victors. Since then a number of investigations, some formal, others informal, have been undertaken regarding the U-65. No satisfactory explanation for any of the strange events that took place on the boat has ever been uncovered. ■

*If you have been timed while reading this selection, enter your reading time below. Then turn to the Words per Minute table on page 155 and look up your reading speed (words per minute). Enter your reading speed on the graph on page 156.*

READING TIME: Unit 17

——————— : ———————
*Minutes*          *Seconds*

# How well did you read?

- *Answer the four types of questions that follow. The directions for each type of question tell you how to mark your answers.*

- *When you have finished all four exercises, check your work by using the answer key on page 152. For each right answer, put a check mark (✔) on the line beside the box. For each wrong answer, write the correct answer on the line.*

- *For scoring each exercise, follow the directions below the questions.*

## A  FINDING THE MAIN IDEA

Look at the three statements below. One expresses the main idea of the story you just read. A good main idea statement answers two questions: it tells *who* or *what* is the subject of the story, and it answers the understood question *does what?* or *is what?* Another statement is *too broad,* it is vague and doesn't tell much about the topic of the story. The third statement is *too narrow,* it tells about only one part of the story.

Match the statements with the three answer choices below by writing the letter of each answer in the box in front of the statement it goes with.

**M—Main Idea     B—Too Broad     N—Too Narrow**

_____ ☐ 1. Several people reported seeing a ghost aboard the U-65, a German submarine used in World War I.

_____ ☐ 2. A great number of strange and tragic events took place aboard a German submarine.

_____ ☐ 3. Tragic events and reported sightings of ghosts plagued a German U-boat right up to its mysterious end.

_____ Score 15 points for a correct *M* answer

_____ Score 5 points for each correct *B* or *N* answer

_____ TOTAL SCORE: Finding the Main Idea

## B RECALLING FACTS

How well do you remember the facts in the story you just read?
Put an *x* in the box in front of the correct answer to each of the
multiple choice questions below.

1. The German U-boats were built in
   - ___ ☐ a. Belgium.
   - ___ ☐ b. France.
   - ___ ☐ c. Germany.

2. Problems started on the U-65
   - ___ ☐ a. when it made its first dive.
   - ___ ☐ b. while it was being built.
   - ___ ☐ c. on launching day.

3. A ghost was first sighted on board the U-65 right after
   - ___ ☐ a. a torpedo explosion.
   - ___ ☐ b. it was launched.
   - ___ ☐ c. its first war patrol.

4. The purpose of an exorcism is to
   - ___ ☐ a. bless a ship before it goes to sea.
   - ___ ☐ b. drive away evil spirits.
   - ___ ☐ c. bring good luck.

5. The U-65 sank
   - ___ ☐ a. when it was torpedoed by an American submarine.
   - ___ ☐ b. as a result of unexplained explosions.
   - ___ ☐ c. after the war ended.

Score 5 points for each correct answer

___ TOTAL SCORE: Recalling Facts

## C MAKING INFERENCES

An inference is a judgment that is made or an idea that is
arrived at based on facts or on information that is given. You
make an inference when you understand something that is *not*
stated directly, but that is *implied*, or suggested by the facts that
are given.

Below are five statements that are judgments or ideas that
have been arrived at from the facts of the story. Write the letter
*C* in the box in front of each statement that is a correct inference. Write the letter *F* in front of each faulty inference.

**C—Correct Inference      F—Faulty Inference**

- ___ ☐ 1. In the first half of World War I, Germany was winning.

- ___ ☐ 2. Admiral Schroeder finally agreed that the U-65 was haunted.

- ___ ☐ 3. The U-65 was a total failure as a weapon.

- ___ ☐ 4. Even Captain Schelle eventually came to believe that the U-65 was cursed.

- ___ ☐ 5. Germany lost World War I largely because of the events that occurred on the U-65.

Score 5 points for each correct answer

___ TOTAL SCORE: Making Inferences

## D USING WORDS PRECISELY

Each of the numbered sentences below contains an underlined word or phrase from the story you have just read. Under the sentence are three definitions. One has the *same* meaning as the underlined word or phrase, one has *almost the same* meaning, and one has the *opposite* meaning. Match the definitions with the three answer choices by writing the letter that stands for each answer in the box in front of the definition it goes with.

**S—Same     A—Almost the Same     O—Opposite**

1. Stories of that sort can quickly <u>demoralize</u> the crew of any warship.

____  ☐ a. encourage

____  ☐ b. weaken the spirit

____  ☐ c. upset

2. Then he <u>broached</u> the subject of the ghost.

____  ☐ a. put aside

____  ☐ b. mentioned

____  ☐ c. brought up

3. After <u>denouncing</u> all talk of jinxed boats and ghosts as "superstitious nonsense," the admiral spent a night on board the U-65.

____  ☐ a. damning

____  ☐ b. rejecting

____  ☐ c. accepting

4. It took several crewmen to subdue the normally <u>imperturbable</u> gunner.

____  ☐ a. excitable

____  ☐ b. cool-headed

____  ☐ c. relaxed

5. For the remainder of the patrol, the crew spent all its time trying to avoid, rather than <u>engage</u>, the enemy.

____  ☐ a. meet

____  ☐ b. join with

____  ☐ c. avoid

____  Score 3 points for each correct S answer

____  Score 1 point for each correct A or O answer

____  TOTAL SCORE: Using Words Precisely

● *Enter the four total scores in the spaces below, and add them together to find your Critical Reading Score. Then record your Critical Reading Score on the graph on page 157.*

_____  Finding the Main Idea
_____  Recalling Facts
_____  Making Inferences
_____  Using Words Precisely

_____  **CRITICAL READING SCORE: Unit 17**

# Lady in Black

On a cold winter night in 1862, a Union soldier shivered in the frigid night air outside Fort Warren. He disliked night patrol at the fort, but he had no choice in the matter. Like all soldiers, he did what he was told. He gazed out at Boston Harbor and gave a melancholy sigh. He hoped that the war between the states would soon be over so that he could return to his family.

As the guard turned to make his return trip along the fort's stockade, he suddenly felt two hands around his neck. Struggling to free himself, he whirled around to confront his attacker and nearly fainted from shock. Facing him was a woman shrouded in black and surrounded by a shimmering halo of eerie light. Her face looked oddly familiar, but before he could remember where he had seen her before, she vanished.

"No one will believe this," the soldier muttered to himself, and he was right. At first his story met with jeers from his comrades. However, when the apparition returned night after night, startling one guard after another, the soldiers stopped laughing. It seemed that Fort Warren was haunted by a lady in black.

* * *

Sarah Lanier tried unsuccessfully to hold back the tears as she waved good-bye to her husband. She and Andrew had grown up together in the little town of Crawfordville, Georgia, and had been childhood sweethearts. Now, only forty-eight hours after their wedding, Andrew was leaving to fight in the Civil War. Like thousands of other young southern men, Lieutenant Lanier had volunteered to fight in the Confederate Army.

Would Sarah ever see Andrew again? She tried not to think about it. Not the type to sit and brood over things beyond her control, she vowed to keep herself busy. She would do her part for the war effort by volunteering at the local hospital, and she would pray for her husband's safe return.

Andrew wrote often, which was some consolation to Sarah. But less than a month after his departure, she received a startling letter. Andrew wrote that he had been captured and was being held prisoner. He was imprisoned along with six hundred other Confederate soldiers, in the Corridor of Dungeons at Fort Warren, on George's Island, off the coast of Boston, Massachusetts.

At least he's still alive, Sarah thought with relief, as she responded vaguely to the sympathy of her family and friends. Already a plan was forming in her mind. She would not sit idle while Andrew suffered in a northern jail. She would go to Boston and try to secure his release.

Horrified at Sarah's plan, her family and friends tried to discourage her. Young southern ladies simply did not travel without chaperones, even in the best of times. Now, with the country at war, she would be in grave danger. Besides, they counseled, her chances of succeeding in freeing her husband were nearly nonexistent.

Refusing to listen to advice, Sarah booked passage on a blockade runner that would take her to Hull, Massachusetts, a seacoast town just a few miles south of Boston. There she would stay with friends who would help her carry out her plans.

Sarah reached her destination two and a half months later. Overlooking Boston Harbor, Hull was the perfect location from which to study Fort Warren, which lay about seven miles off the mainland in Boston Harbor. Using a telescope, Sarah was able to identify the Corridor of Dungeons, where her husband was imprisoned. She studied the height of the prison walls and their distance from the shore, and noted where the guards were stationed and when they patrolled.

On a bitter January night, with sleet falling relentlessly, Sarah put her plan into action. Her hair cut short, and wearing a man's dark suit, she climbed

*Sarah Lanier was a strong-willed woman, determined to rescue her young husband from the dismal Corridor of Dungeons at Fort Warren. For her attempt, Sarah paid with her life. There are many who say that Sarah's spirit never left the fort.*

into a small boat and was rowed by her friends across Hingham Bay into Boston Harbor. After she had been dropped off at George's Island, Sarah crouched in the surf, waiting for the guards to pass by. She timed their patrol a second time for good measure; there was no room for mistakes now. Sarah calculated that she had a minute and a half to scramble the two or three hundred feet across the beach and into the bushes at the base of the stockade. After the guards passed again, she would have another ninety seconds to clamber over the stockade and drop into the courtyard of the fort.

Thankful for the sleet that helped to camouflage her, Sarah made it across the wet sand to the bushes. Her heart thudded as she waited for the guards to pass. Then she scaled the stockade and landed with a thump on the other side. She was inside the fort, with her husband only yards away in the Corridor of Dungeons.

After checking to be certain there were no sentries within earshot, Sarah began to whistle a tune she was sure her husband would recognize—the melody of an old folk song they had sung together since childhood. Failing to get an answer, Sarah whistled the tune again, but still she heard no answer.

For the first time since she resolved to

rescue her husband, Sarah began to have doubts about her scheme. While she was traveling north, there had been no way she could have gotten word from Andrew. He might be sick, or perhaps he had even been transferred to another prison. In a last desperate attempt, Sarah whistled a third time. She waited what seemed like an eternity. Then she heard faintly, mingled with the patter of falling sleet, the softly whistled notes of the old folk tune. Andrew was there!

Sarah watched as a crude ladder made from blankets tied together came hurtling over the wall. Grasping hold, she was hoisted over the wall and into her husband's waiting arms. The other prisoners listened with amazement as Sarah related her incredible story. Then from under her clothing she pulled a bundle containing a pick, a shovel, a pistol, and a box of ammunition. With the tools they could tunnel under the walls of the fort to freedom.

But the prisoners suggested another course of action: instead of escaping, they wanted to tunnel into the courtyard near the guard post, surprise the guard, and seize the fort. From there, they might even occupy the city of Boston! They went ahead with that plan.

Days and then weeks passed, and little by little the tunnel grew. Sarah and the men scattered some of the excavated dirt outside the fortress walls; the rest they hid in their blankets and clothing. Finally they reached a point that they determined

was in the center of the courtyard. But when they swung the pick to break through to the surface, the metal clanged against stone wall; they had miscalculated. Alerted by the sound, a sentry called out the garrison, and the guards soon discovered the tunnel and the prisoners' plan.

But the Union soldiers knew nothing about Sarah Lanier, who remained hidden in the tunnel as the Confederate prisoners were rounded up and counted. At the proper moment, she intended to sneak up behind the colonel and catch him unaware, giving the prisoners the chance to turn on the guards and take the fort. Unfortunately for Sarah and the Confederate soldiers, the daring plan backfired. When Sarah held a pistol to the colonel's back, he calmly ordered his troops to surround her. Confused and hesitant, Sarah allowed the colonel to snatch her pistol, causing it to go off. She watched in horror as Andrew crumpled to the ground, killed instantly by the stray bullet.

Sobbing, Sarah ran to her husband. The Union soldiers were astonished to discover that she was a woman. Nevertheless, she was a spy and must receive the established punishment for spying: death by hanging.

The colonel must have felt some pity for the courageous woman, for he granted Sarah's last request. She expressed a wish to be hanged in clothes befitting a southern lady, so the colonel provided a long black robe that he found in the fort.

Wearing the black robe, and managing a brave smile, Sarah walked to the gallows on the morning of February 2, 1862. Several hours later, her body was cut down and buried next to that of her husband.

Sarah's body may have been put to rest, but it seems that her spirit was not. Since her first appearance to sentries patrolling the stockade at Fort Warren seven weeks after her hanging, the Lady in Black has appeared many times. One sentry who patrolled the fort during World War II was literally frightened out of his wits by the apparition; to this day he remains in a mental hospital.

Today Fort Warren is no longer used as a prison. It is a historic site and a popular tourist attraction. The bodies of Sarah and Andrew Lanier have long since been removed to Georgia, yet, they say that late at night the ghost of the Lady in Black continues to haunt the old fort that sits in Boston Harbor. ∎

*If you have been timed while reading this selection, enter your reading time below. Then turn to the Words per Minute table on page 155 and look up your reading speed (words per minute). Enter your reading speed on the graph on page 156.*

**READING TIME: Unit 18**

———————— : ————————
*Minutes*          *Seconds*

# How well did you read?

- *Answer the four types of questions that follow. The directions for each type of question tell you how to mark your answers.*

- *When you have finished all four exercises, check your work by using the answer key on page 152. For each right answer, put a check mark (✔) on the line beside the box. For each wrong answer, write the correct answer on the line.*

- *For scoring each exercise, follow the directions below the questions.*

## A  FINDING THE MAIN IDEA

Look at the three statements below. One expresses the main idea of the story you just read. A good main idea statement answers two questions: it tells *who* or *what* is the subject of the story, and it answers the understood question *does what?* or *is what?* Another statement is *too broad*, it is vague and doesn't tell much about the topic of the story. The third statement is *too narrow*, it tells about only one part of the story.

Match the statements with the three answer choices below by writing the letter of each answer in the box in front of the statement it goes with.

**M—Main Idea**      **B—Too Broad**      **N—Too Narrow**

_____ ☐ 1. Sarah Lanier was hanged when she was found to be a spy.

_____ ☐ 2. A ghost shrouded in black supposedly haunts a fort that sits on an island in Boston Harbor.

_____ ☐ 3. It is said that the ghost of a southern woman who was hanged as a spy during the Civil War still haunts the prison where she was killed.

_____ Score 15 points for a correct *M* answer

_____ Score 5 points for each correct *B* or *N* answer

_____ TOTAL SCORE: Finding the Main Idea

## B RECALLING FACTS

How well do you remember the facts in the story you just read?
Put an *x* in the box in front of the correct answer to each of the
multiple choice questions below.

1. Fort Warren is situated
   - ☐ a. in the Corridor of Dungeons.
   - ☐ b. on George's Island.
   - ☐ c. in Boston, Massachusetts.

2. To let Andrew know she was outside the prison walls, Sarah
   - ☐ a. sang a childhood song.
   - ☐ b. whistled an old folk tune.
   - ☐ c. threw a rock over the wall.

3. The Confederate prisoners decided to
   - ☐ a. dig a tunnel under the wall of the fort to the outside.
   - ☐ b. try to seize the fort.
   - ☐ c. dig a tunnel to Boston.

4. Sarah's last request was to be
   - ☐ a. hanged in clothes fit for a lady.
   - ☐ b. buried next to her husband.
   - ☐ c. hanged rather than shot.

5. Sarah and Andrew are now buried
   - ☐ a. at Fort Warren.
   - ☐ b. in Georgia.
   - ☐ c. in Boston.

Score 5 points for each correct answer

_____ TOTAL SCORE: Recalling Facts

## C MAKING INFERENCES

An inference is a judgment that is made or an idea that is
arrived at based on facts or on information that is given. You
make an inference when you understand something that is *not*
stated directly, but that is *implied,* or suggested by the facts that
are given.

Below are five statements that are judgments or ideas that
have been arrived at from the facts of the story. Write the letter
*C* in the box in front of each statement that is a correct inference. Write the letter *F* in front of each faulty inference.

**C—Correct Inference      F—Faulty Inference**

1. ☐ Spies today are still usually punished by hanging.

2. ☐ Fort Warren is no longer used as a prison because too many guards were badly frightened by the ghost of the Lady in Black.

3. ☐ Had they followed Sarah's plan, the Confederate prisoners would have had a good chance of escaping.

4. ☐ The Confederate prisoners cared more about their duty as soldiers than about their personal safety.

5. ☐ Andrew was prepared for Sarah's arrival at the prison.

Score 5 points for each correct answer

_____ TOTAL SCORE: Making Inferences

## D USING WORDS PRECISELY

Each of the numbered sentences below contains an underlined word or phrase from the story you have just read. Under the sentence are three definitions. One has the *same* meaning as the underlined word or phrase, one has *almost the same* meaning, and one has the *opposite* meaning. Match the definitions with the three answer choices by writing the letter that stands for each answer in the box in front of the definition it goes with.

**S—Same      A—Almost the Same      O—Opposite**

1. He gazed out at Boston Harbor and gave a melancholy sigh.

—— ☐ a. gloomy

—— ☐ b. lighthearted

—— ☐ c. sullen

2. Struggling to free himself, he whirled around to confront his attacker and nearly fainted from shock.

—— ☐ a. meet

—— ☐ b. face

—— ☐ c. avoid

3. At first his story met with jeers from his comrades.

—— ☐ a. laughs

—— ☐ b. mockery

—— ☐ c. cheers

4. Not the type to sit and brood over things beyond her control, she vowed to keep herself busy.

—— ☐ a. sulk

—— ☐ b. rejoice

—— ☐ c. worry

5. For the first time since she resolved to rescue her husband, Sarah began to have doubts about her scheme.

—— ☐ a. decided

—— ☐ b. proposed

—— ☐ c. hesitated

—— Score 3 points for each correct S answer

—— Score 1 point for each correct A or O answer

—— TOTAL SCORE: Using Words Precisely

● *Enter the four total scores in the spaces below, and add them together to find your Critical Reading Score. Then record your Critical Reading Score on the graph on page 157.*

———— Finding the Main Idea

———— Recalling Facts

———— Making Inferences

———— Using Words Precisely

———— CRITICAL READING SCORE: Unit 18

# The Yankee Poltergeist

What was it about the Reverend Eliakim Phelps and his family that attracted one of the most vicious spirits of all time? The reverend *had* been known to dabble in the occult on occasion—he had tried to contact spirits from the "other world," and had also attempted to treat diseases through hypnosis. But in the mid-1800s, interest in the supernatural was sweeping the United States. Many mediums, some of whom were later revealed to be frauds, claimed to be able to contact the dead. Therefore, it was not considered terribly unusual that the good reverend should hold a belief in spiritualism. In the eyes of his congregation in the village of Stratford, Connecticut, Dr. Phelps was a model clergyman.

From all outward appearances, his family was happy and normal. Dr. Phelps, who was nearly sixty years old, had recently married a young widow with four children—two girls and two boys. Mrs. Phelps and her children were a lively addition to the Stratford manse. Yet it was in the midst of this family that a most horrifying supernatural presence chose to establish itself, turning their pleasant existence into a nightmare.

It started on March 4, 1840, when a friend of Dr. Phelps's, visiting from New York, suggested that he and the reverend attempt to contact spirits by holding a séance. Dr. Phelps agreed. Although the men heard some faint rappings, they were otherwise disappointed with the results. Six days later, however, they got an unpleasant surprise.

On Sunday, March 10, the Phelps family went to church as usual. What they found when they returned home gave all of them an incredible shock. The house had been totally disrupted. Furniture was overturned and scattered throughout the rooms, books had been flung from the shelves, and closets had been opened and disarranged. It appeared to have been the work of burglars, except for one curious thing: someone had taken pieces of clothing and laid them on the floor in the forms of eleven figures, arranged in what appeared to be some kind of religious ceremony. Bibles placed near the figures were opened to passages referring to ghosts.

That was only the first of many bizarre artistic creations. Although the house was watched carefully, during the following week thirty more works of art appeared. According to an article in the *New Haven Journal*, some of them were "most beautiful and picturesque." Witnesses concluded that a supernatural agency was at work.

The Stratford Poltergeist, as the spirit came to be called, was only warming up.

*Poltergeist*, a German word meaning "noisy ghost," is the name given to a supernatural presence that launches loud and often violent attacks. This presence certainly earned its name, turning the Phelps home, in a matter of days, into a madhouse.

Dr. Phelps tried to communicate with the spirit. Although his first attempts failed, he continued to try. He asked the spirit questions. It was not long before he received answers, in the form of raps—one rap meant "yes," and two raps meant "no." When the spirit began to talk, however, he stopped asking questions and ordered his family to do the same, for the answers were often shockingly crude.

Soon, even more outrageous events began to take place. Visitors saw members of the family carried across the room by an invisible force and deposited on the floor. Furniture was tipped over when no one was in the room. Professor Austin Phelps, Dr. Phelps's son by his first marriage, described several experiences: "In the presence of the whole family, a turnip fell from the ceiling. Spoons and forks flew from the dinner table into the air, and one day six or eight spoons were taken up at once, bent double by no visible agency, and thrown at those in the room."

On another occasion the family watched

as a "vegetable growth" suddenly appeared on the sitting-room carpet. It spread as if it were alive, and strange symbols formed on its leaves. Then the whole thing vanished.

A reporter from the *New Haven Journal* witnessed a huge porcelain jug hurled against a door with such force that it left a large dent. The reporter noted a curious fact: the jug did not fly in a straight line from where it had rested, but in a semicircle.

Sometimes the spirit communicated in writing. Messages were scrawled on walls, and letters were dropped from the ceilings. One day, when Dr. Phelps was writing at a table, he was interrupted for a moment. When he sat down to resume his work, he discovered strange marks and writing on the paper, the ink still wet to the touch.

The poltergeist could also be frighteningly vicious. Mrs. Phelps's sixteen-year-old daughter was once almost smothered by a pillow while she slept. On another occasion she was nearly strangled by a tape that suddenly wrapped itself around her neck. A reporter for the *New York Sun* saw a fresh red mark on the girl's arm, the result of a cruel pinch from the spirit. The same reporter, along with several other witnesses, watched a matchbox fall from a mantel and slide under the bed of one of the boys. The boy then jumped up,

*The spirit made odd and beautiful works of art. It also tormented people, threw things, and spoke crudely and menacingly. It even caused bizarre objects to materialize from nowhere. Those who encountered the poltergeist, as it came to be known, were mystified. Just what terrible spirit was it that the Reverend Eliakim Phelps had accidentally called into his house to terrify his family?*

claiming he was on fire. The reporter found a flaming scrap of paper beneath the bed.

In an attempt to stop the grotesque and violent occurrences, Dr. Phelps resumed communication with the spirit, which seemed happy to oblige. A strange story emerged, in which the ghost claimed to be the spirit of a Frenchman who had worked as a law clerk. The spirit admitted to once drawing up some papers for Mrs. Phelps, in which he cheated her out of some money. When Dr. Phelps studied the papers in question, he quickly discovered that there had indeed been a fraud.

Was the spirit who it claimed to be? Andrew Jackson Davis, a famous young psychic who went to investigate the Phelps haunting, had other ideas. After examining the Phelps household, he concluded that most of the strange events were the result of what he called "magnetic charges" from the two oldest Phelps children. The children were given to sudden changes in radiation, the psychic explained, similar to an alternating current of electricity. Objects were either repelled by or attracted to them, depending on the radiation. The psychic did not omit the possibility of a ghost altogether, however. He claimed that spirits were also involved, and that he himself had seen five. The fanfare with which Davis announced his conclusions added great glamour to the haunting, and a lot of publicity ensued.

It did nothing to ease the frenzied lives of the Phelps family.

In October, after eighteen months of chaos, Dr. Phelps sent his family to Pennsylvania for a rest. The hauntings stopped immediately, and calm prevailed for the five weeks that Dr. Phelps lived alone there. When the family returned to Stratford the following spring, all remained peaceful.

What caused the Stratford Poltergeist? Were spirits at work? Was the whole episode, as Davis suggested, the result of magnetic forces? Was it a case of fraud on the part of one or more persons in the Phelps household? Although the events have been studied by a number of investigators, both at the time and after the fact, no evidence was ever produced to support a single theory.

It seems unlikely, however, that anyone in the Phelps family participated in such an elaborate hoax. If Dr. Phelps was the trickster, then he certainly lost much more than he gained. Not only was his life disrupted, but he suffered financially as well. In an interview, he claimed to have lost "between one and two hundred dollars—while the spirit messages were valueless! Twenty window-panes broken . . . servants lost, valuable articles destroyed. . . ." What's more, there is no explanation for why a respectable minister should want to promote such a grand deception.

Mrs. Phelps, an educated woman, active in church affairs, also seems an unlikely perpetrator of a scam. As for the children, Phelps dismissed their being part of a fraud as "wholly inadmissible." The fantastic occurrences, he claimed, were "absolutely inexplicable." "Fifty-six articles," he said, "were picked up at one time and thrown at someone's head. . . . Heavy marble-topped tables would rise on two legs and crash to the floor with no one within six feet of them. . . ."

Witnesses to many of the events, including friends, neighbors, three reporters, and four members of the clergy, agreed that no member of the household could have tricked them.

Whatever caused the Stratford Poltergeist, there is no denying the fact that for eighteen months an incredible series of disturbing events took place that no one, to this day, has been able to explain. ■

*If you have been timed while reading this selection, enter your reading time below. Then turn to the Words per Minute table on page 155 and look up your reading speed (words per minute). Enter your reading speed on the graph on page 156.*

---

READING TIME: Unit 19

_____ : _____
*Minutes*          *Seconds*

# How well did you read?

- *Answer the four types of questions that follow. The directions for each type of question tell you how to mark your answers.*

- *When you have finished all four exercises, check your work by using the answer key on page 152. For each right answer, put a check mark (✔) on the line beside the box. For each wrong answer, write the correct answer on the line.*

- *For scoring each exercise, follow the directions below the questions.*

## A  FINDING THE MAIN IDEA

Look at the three statements below. One expresses the main idea of the story you just read. A good main idea statement answers two questions: it tells *who* or *what* is the subject of the story, and it answers the understood question *does what?* or *is what?* Another statement is *too broad*, it is vague and doesn't tell much about the topic of the story. The third statement is *too narrow*, it tells about only one part of the story.

Match the statements with the three answer choices below by writing the letter of each answer in the box in front of the statement it goes with.

**M—Main Idea     B—Too Broad     N—Too Narrow**

_____ ☐ 1. A vicious, unexplained spirit haunted the Phelps house for eighteen months.

_____ ☐ 2. Dr. Phelps was interested in the occult and had tried on various occasions to contact spirits.

_____ ☐ 3. In the mid-1800s, wild occurrences disturbed the Phelps family.

_____ Score 15 points for a correct *M* answer
_____ Score 5 points for each correct *B* or *N* answer

_____ TOTAL SCORE: Finding the Main Idea

133

## B RECALLING FACTS

How well do you remember the facts in the story you just read? Put an x in the box in front of the correct answer to each of the multiple choice questions below.

1. The poltergeist started disturbing the Phelps household in
   ___ ☐ a. 1830.
   ___ ☐ b. 1840.
   ___ ☐ c. 1850.

2. The poltergeist made its first visit
   ___ ☐ a. while the Phelps family was in church.
   ___ ☐ b. during a séance.
   ___ ☐ c. while the Phelps family was eating dinner.

3. The word *poltergeist* means
   ___ ☐ a. violent spirit.
   ___ ☐ b. evil presence.
   ___ ☐ c. noisy ghost.

4. At one point the spirit claimed to be
   ___ ☐ a. Dr. Phelps's father.
   ___ ☐ b. a friend of Mrs. Phelps.
   ___ ☐ c. a dishonest law clerk.

5. Andrew Jackson Davis concluded that the strange activities were the result of
   ___ ☐ a. radiation from the sun.
   ___ ☐ b. magnetic charges.
   ___ ☐ c. alternating currents of electricity.

Score 5 points for each correct answer

___ TOTAL SCORE: Recalling Facts

## C MAKING INFERENCES

An inference is a judgment that is made or an idea that is arrived at based on facts or on information that is given. You make an inference when you understand something that is *not* stated directly, but that is *implied,* or suggested by the facts that are given.

Below are five statements that are judgments or ideas that have been arrived at from the facts of the story. Write the letter *C* in the box in front of each statement that is a correct inference. Write the letter *F* in front of each faulty inference.

**C—Correct Inference     F—Faulty Inference**

___ ☐ 1. Dr. Phelps was upset with the poltergeist mainly because of the damage the spirit had done to his home.

___ ☐ 2. Andrew Jackson Davis enjoyed publicity.

___ ☐ 3. The newspapers made up many stories about the Phelps family and the poltergeist.

___ ☐ 4. The disturbances in the Phelps household were big news at the time they were taking place.

___ ☐ 5. Dr. Phelps was quite well-to-do.

Score 5 points for each correct answer

___ TOTAL SCORE: Making Inferences

# D USING WORDS PRECISELY

Each of the numbered sentences below contains an underlined word or phrase from the story you have just read. Under the sentence are three definitions. One has the *same* meaning as the underlined word or phrase, one has *almost the same* meaning, and one has the *opposite* meaning. Match the definitions with the three answer choices by writing the letter that stands for each answer in the box in front of the definition it goes with.

**S—Same     A—Almost the Same     O—Opposite**

1. The fanfare with which Davis announced his conclusions added great glamour to the haunting, and a lot of publicity ensued.

     ☐ a. took place

     ☐ b. led the way

     ☐ c. resulted

2. It did nothing to ease the frenzied lives of the Phelps family.

     ☐ a. calm

     ☐ b. agitated

     ☐ c. disorderly

3. The hauntings stopped immediately, and calm prevailed.

     ☐ a. survived

     ☐ b. lasted

     ☐ c. ended

4. Mrs. Phelps, an educated woman, active in church affairs, also seems an unlikely perpetrator of a scam.

     ☐ a. source

     ☐ b. receiver

     ☐ c. creator

5. As for the children, Phelps dismissed their being part of a fraud as "wholly inadmissible."

     ☐ a. rejected

     ☐ b. eliminated

     ☐ c. accepted

____ Score 3 points for each correct *S* answer
____ Score 1 point for each correct *A* or *O* answer

____ TOTAL SCORE: Using Words Precisely

● *Enter the four total scores in the spaces below, and add them together to find your Critical Reading Score. Then record your Critical Reading Score on the graph on page 157.*

| | |
|---|---|
| _____ | Finding the Main Idea |
| _____ | Recalling Facts |
| _____ | Making Inferences |
| _____ | Using Words Precisely |
| _____ | **CRITICAL READING SCORE: Unit 19** |

William Briggs was a respected man, generally regarded as honest. So when he testified in court regarding a conversation he'd had with his friend Thomas Harris, the judge had a difficult time determining what was true. The problem was, Thomas Harris was dead at the time of the conversation.

# Testimony of a Ghost in Court

William Briggs shifted uncomfortably in the witness chair as Robert Wright, counsel for the plaintiff, continued his questioning. "You say you saw your friend Thomas Harris walking toward you that morning?" Wright exclaimed with disbelief in his voice. "That's correct, sir," Briggs affirmed. "Surely you must have been mistaken," said Wright. "Is it not a matter of public record that Thomas Harris died several months before? In fact, were you not present at his bedside when he died?" "Yes, I was with Tom when he died," said Mr. Briggs. "Nevertheless, the figure I saw that day was definitely Tom. He was wearing his sky-blue suit, the one he wore when he was last in health, and he walked toward me, as if he had something important to say." "You would have us believe then, sir, that you had an encounter with Tom Harris's ghost?" asked Wright incredulously.

As low murmurs rippled through the gallery, the Honorable James Tilghman rapped his gavel for silence. "Quiet in the courtroom!" he demanded.

If it had come from anyone else, the story William Briggs told in court would have seemed too incredible to be believed. But Briggs, then forty-three years old and a veteran of the Revolutionary War, was a respected person in Queen Anne's County, Maryland. He was certainly not the kind of person to make up a preposterous ghost story.

"Let the witness continue his testimony," ordered Judge Tilghman. Briggs went on to tell about the day that he had been riding in the vicinity of the lot where his best friend lay buried, when his horse, which had once belonged to Harris, suddenly began to walk very fast. Briggs looked around carefully, but could discover nothing that might have startled the animal. The morning was sunny, and they were alone on the road, yet the horse was obviously disturbed by something. As they turned into a lane that ran near Harris's grave, the horse whirled around, went to the fence surrounding the lot, and stood looking in the direction of his former master's grave. The horse neighed loudly.

At that moment, Briggs saw Tom Harris, dressed in his favorite sky-blue coat, walking toward him. Just before he reached the fence, Harris turned sharply and disappeared.

That occurred in March of 1790, Briggs affirmed. Three months later, in June, he had another experience involving Thomas Harris's ghost. It took place while he was plowing his field, which was some three miles from the plot of ground in which Tom Harris lay buried. Briggs testified that it was early twilight when Harris, wearing the same blue coat, suddenly appeared alongside him and walked with him for about two hundred yards. Harris stopped as if he was going to speak, but when Briggs's helper, John Bailey, came toward them, the ghost vanished. No, said Briggs, Bailey had not seen the ghost, and Briggs had not mentioned the matter to him.

Briggs said that that occurrence made him so uneasy that his health was affected. He was convinced that his old friend had come back to convey an important message, but in two visits nothing had been said. Other strange happenings followed. One night Briggs heard a loud groan, which he said sounded exactly like the noise Harris had made just before he died. Briggs's wife also heard the groan, and although they searched the house thoroughly, they found nothing. On another night Briggs was awakened by a blow on the face that blackened both his eyes and left him with a swollen nose.

Harris finally made another appearance when Briggs was alone in his field on a clear, starlit night in August. The apparition came up to him, stretched out his arms and rested them on Briggs's shoulders. Briggs said he felt no pressure, and in a moment the ghost was gone. Again, no word was spoken.

In October, about eight o'clock in the morning, Briggs and John Bailey were working together in the farmyard when Briggs saw Tom Harris walking along the garden fence only a few feet away. Before Briggs could call out to Bailey, however, the ghost disappeared. Two hours later, the apparition was back, leaning over the fence about ten feet from where Briggs was working. "Look there!" Briggs cried excitedly to Bailey. Bailey looked curiously at his employer, for he saw nothing but air. "Don't you see Harris?" Briggs insisted. Then he walked to the fence, climbed over it, and walked up to the shade of his old friend.

At last the ghost began to talk. At first its voice was so low and it spoke so rapidly that Briggs had trouble following what it was saying, but slowly the voice became clearer, and Briggs was able to understand what Harris wanted. In his will, Harris had ordered that his land be sold and the profits divided among his four children. However, when the lawyer drew up the deed of sale, he discovered a law that made Harris's wishes illegal. The law stated that a man could not leave his land to anyone but his heirs. Since Harris's four children were illegitimate, they could not inherit the property or any money from its sale. As a result, Thomas's

brother James, who was Thomas's next of kin, received the estate. The children would receive nothing. Tom Harris's ghost had returned to make sure his children received what was rightfully theirs.

"Ask my brother if he does not remember the conversation which passed between us on the east side of the wheat stacks the day I was taken with my death sickness," said the ghost. "I wish all my property should be kept together by James until my children are of age. Then the whole should be sold and divided among them; not now. The children will be most needful of the property while they are minors." Harris wanted his children to be able to continue to live on the property until they were grown, and then to receive the profits from its sale. He had left it to his brother to honor those wishes.

Briggs immediately went to see James Harris, Thomas's brother, and told him what had occurred. When Briggs recounted his conversation with the ghost, James was convinced that Briggs was speaking the truth. "No one on earth but he and I knew of that conversation," James admitted. Then he promised to carry out his brother's wishes.

Unfortunately, James Harris died soon afterward, before he had a chance to carry out his promise. His widow then inherited

Thomas Harris's estate, and refused to give up what she considered to have been her husband's lawful inheritance. A suit was brought against her on behalf of Tom Harris's four children.

William Briggs was called in to testify in the court case, which took place in 1798 or 1799 in Queen Anne's County, Maryland. Despite the fact that he was the only person to claim to have seen the ghost of Tom Harris, his testimony was accepted by the court. And while the records are unclear, it appears to have been his testimony about his conversation with Thomas Harris's ghost that settled the issue in favor of Harris's children. ■

*If you have been timed while reading this selection, enter your reading time below. Then turn to the Words per Minute table on page 155 and look up your reading speed (words per minute). Enter your reading speed on the graph on page 156.*

**READING TIME: Unit 20**

_____ : _____
*Minutes*      *Seconds*

# How well did you read?

- *Answer the four types of questions that follow. The directions for each type of question tell you how to mark your answers.*

- *When you have finished all four exercises, check your work by using the answer key on page 152. For each right answer, put a check mark (✔) on the line beside the box. For each wrong answer, write the correct answer on the line.*

- *For scoring each exercise, follow the directions below the questions.*

## A   FINDING THE MAIN IDEA

Look at the three statements below. One expresses the main idea of the story you just read. A good main idea statement answers two questions: it tells *who* or *what* is the subject of the story, and it answers the understood question *does what?* or *is what?* Another statement is *too broad,* it is vague and doesn't tell much about the topic of the story. The third statement is *too narrow,* it tells about only one part of the story.

Match the statements with the three answer choices below by writing the letter of each answer in the box in front of the statement it goes with.

**M—Main Idea      B—Too Broad      N—Too Narrow**

_____  ☐ 1. Testimony based on a supposed conversation with a ghost appears to have decided the outcome of a court case.

_____  ☐ 2. The supposed word of a ghost was accepted in a legal battle.

_____  ☐ 3. William Briggs claimed to have had a conversation with the ghost of his friend Tom Harris.

_____ Score 15 points for a correct *M* answer

_____ Score 5 points for each correct *B* or *N* answer

_____ TOTAL SCORE: Finding the Main Idea

## B  RECALLING FACTS

How well do you remember the facts in the story you just read?
Put an *x* in the box in front of the correct answer to each of the
multiple choice questions below.

1. William Briggs claimed that he first saw the ghost of
   Tom Harris
   ___ ☐ a. in his cornfield.
   ___ ☐ b. near Harris's grave.
   ___ ☐ c. in the farmyard.

2. The will said that Tom Harris's property should be
   ___ ☐ a. sold and the profits divided among Harris's
           children.
   ___ ☐ b. kept for Harris's children and sold when they
           were grown.
   ___ ☐ c. sold and the profits given to Harris's brother
           for safekeeping.

3. Tom Harris's ghost was seen by
   ___ ☐ a. William Briggs and James Harris.
   ___ ☐ b. William Briggs and John Bailey.
   ___ ☐ c. William Briggs.

4. A law suit was brought against
   ___ ☐ a. James Harris.
   ___ ☐ b. the widow of James Harris.
   ___ ☐ c. the children of Tom Harris.

5. Tom Harris spoke to his brother about his will
   ___ ☐ a. the day he became seriously ill.
   ___ ☐ b. the day he died.
   ___ ☐ c. the day before he died.


Score 5 points for each correct answer

___ TOTAL SCORE: Recalling Facts

## C  MAKING INFERENCES

An inference is a judgment that is made or an idea that is
arrived at based on facts or on information that is given. You
make an inference when you understand something that is *not*
stated directly, but that is *implied,* or suggested by the facts that
are given.

Below are five statements that are judgments or ideas that
have been arrived at from the facts of the story. Write the letter
*C* in the box in front of each statement that is a correct inference. Write the letter *F* in front of each faulty inference.

**C—Correct Inference      F—Faulty Inference**

___ ☐ 1. The testimony of William Briggs was accepted
         because no one doubted his word.

___ ☐ 2. William Briggs made up the ghost story to
         protect Tom Harris's children.

___ ☐ 3. James and Tom Harris did not get along well.

___ ☐ 4. Tom Harris trusted his brother James.

___ ☐ 5. The ghost of Tom Harris appeared because his
         wishes were not being carried out.


Score 5 points for each correct answer

___ TOTAL SCORE: Making Inferences

## D USING WORDS PRECISELY

Each of the numbered sentences below contains an underlined word or phrase from the story you have just read. Under the sentence are three definitions. One has the *same* meaning as the underlined word or phrase, one has *almost the same* meaning, and one has the *opposite* meaning. Match the definitions with the three answer choices by writing the letter that stands for each answer in the box in front of the definition it goes with.

**S—Same     A—Almost the Same     O—Opposite**

1. "You would have us believe then, sir, that you had an encounter with Tom Harris's ghost?" asked Wright incredulously.

____ ☐ a. with disbelief

____ ☐ b. acceptingly

____ ☐ c. doubtfully

2. "That's correct, sir," Briggs affirmed.

____ ☐ a. denied

____ ☐ b. declared

____ ☐ c. verified

3. He was certainly not the kind of person to make up a preposterous ghost story.

____ ☐ a. outrageous

____ ☐ b. silly

____ ☐ c. sensible

4. He was convinced that his old friend had come back to convey an important message, but in two visits nothing had been said.

____ ☐ a. deliver

____ ☐ b. receive

____ ☐ c. carry

5. He had left it to his brother to honor those wishes.

____ ☐ a. ignore

____ ☐ b. carry out

____ ☐ c. respect

____ Score 3 points for each correct S answer
____ Score 1 point for each correct A or O answer

____ **TOTAL SCORE: Using Words Precisely**

● *Enter the four total scores in the spaces below, and add them together to find your Critical Reading Score. Then record your Critical Reading Score on the graph on page 157.*

____ Finding the Main Idea
____ Recalling Facts
____ Making Inferences
____ Using Words Precisely
____ **CRITICAL READING SCORE: Unit 20**

# Spiritualism: Fact or Fraud?

Spiritualism—the belief that a person's spirit survives after death and can communicate with the living through a medium—got its start on Friday, March 31, 1848. On that day two young girls, Margaret and Katherine Fox, reported having the first of a number of "spirit conversations." Those conversations were to make the Fox family, and spiritualism, the talk of the country.

In December of 1847, the Fox family moved into a house in the small town of Hydesville, in upstate New York. Within two months strange rappings began to be heard at all hours—but only when the two girls were present. Margaret and Katherine—or Kate, as she was called—were not at all upset by the noises.

Their parents, on the other hand, were distressed, especially their mother, who was a devout Methodist. She was convinced that the sounds were the work of the devil. Hearing that, Margaret and Kate laughingly named the phenomenon "Mr. Splitfoot," because the devil is often pictured as having cloven hooves.

Mrs. Fox tried unsuccessfully to find the source of the rappings. Then, on March 31, after the family had gone to bed, the rappings started up and were so persistent that no one could sleep. One of the children finally sat up in bed and called out, "Here, Mr. Splitfoot, do as I do." She snapped her fingers once and was answered with a single rap. She then snapped her fingers several more times, and was answered with an equal number of raps.

By that time the girls' parents had joined them. Together they worked out a simple code. Phrasing questions that could be answered with a yes or no or a number, Mrs. Fox interrogated the knocking intruder. It answered all her questions correctly.

The Foxes were informed that Mr. Splitfoot was the spirit of a man who in life had been a peddler. He had supposedly been robbed of five hundred dollars, murdered in that very house, and buried in the cellar.

The next day the Foxes tried to check out the story. Town records held no mention of any peddlers being murdered, nor did a search of the cellar yield any bones. What did get out, however, was news of the rappings. Before long the house was crowded with curious folks from all over the Northeast.

The excitement in the Fox house became so great that Mrs. Fox sent Margaret and Kate to live with their older sister, Leah, in Rochester. Mrs. Fox hoped that the spirit would not follow the girls, but it did.

Since Rochester was a big city, once the news of Mr. Splitfoot got out even greater crowds converged on the Fox sisters. Soon all three sisters were the center of a devoted "spirit circle," which met nightly in Leah's house.

Soon the shrewd Leah, who was more than twenty years older than her sisters, conceived the idea of making money from the phenomenon. She arranged a public demonstration in Corinthian Hall, Rochester's largest auditorium. Admission was set at one dollar, a tidy sum in those days.

The "rapping telegraph," as the question-and-answer system was dubbed, was a rousing success. Two more meetings were held, both before packed houses. Not everyone was taken with the show, however. Some people set out to prove that the Fox sisters were frauds.

Committees were formed to study the performances. Nothing dishonest was discovered. Still, enraged doubters began throwing firecrackers onto the stage and threatening the sisters. The police hustled the women to safety.

The sisters began touring, attracting large crowds wherever they performed. They also offered private demonstrations. Their clients included the rich and the famous. Among them was Mary Todd Lincoln, who wished to communicate with her recently assassinated husband, President Abraham Lincoln.

As spiritualism spread, arguments for and against it raged. The believers far outnumbered the nonbelievers. Indeed, the harder the skeptics tried to discredit the Fox sisters, the more firmly their supporters believed.

Then, on October 21, 1888—forty years after the first incidents at Hydesville—Margaret Fox gave a special demonstration at the Academy of Music in New York City. Her purpose: to confess to defrauding the public. A newspaper account of the day describes the reaction of the audience to the news:

> There was a dead silence; everybody in the hall knew they were looking upon the woman who is principally responsible for spiritualism. She stood upon a little pine table, with nothing on her feet but stockings. As she remained motionless, loud distinct rappings were heard, now in the flies, now behind the scenes, now in the gallery.

Margaret was making the rapping sounds by snapping a joint in her big toe. The acoustical properties of the hall gave the illusion that the sounds were coming from different locations.

You might think that this astonishing

*The Fox sisters and Leonora Piper were big names in spiritualism during the late 1800s and early 1900s. They claimed to be able to communicate with the dead. The Fox sisters performed in public for years. They had many devoted followers. In fact, they were responsible for the start of the whole spiritualist movement. Leonora Piper regularly entered into trances during which spirits supposedly spoke through her. Are there really people who can communicate with spirits, or are such demonstrations purely tricks? You'll have to decide for yourself.*

revelation spelled the end of spiritualism, but it didn't. People refused to believe Margaret. They argued that she had been forced into a false confession—by the churches, perhaps, or by the newspapers. And even if the Fox sisters were frauds, they argued, that did not mean that all spiritualists were frauds.

Two years later, the sisters retracted the confession and took up their demonstrations once again. Both Margaret and Kate, however, were deep in the grip of alcoholism and died soon after. Only the wily Leah was able to go on, and she did, amassing a small fortune.

Given that story, you might reasonably conclude that spiritualism was a hoax. But before you make up your mind, consider the story of Leonora Piper.

In 1884 Leonora Piper, plagued by a series of ailments, sought relief from a psychic healer in Boston. Though her first visit offered no relief, Leonora later said that some powerful force commanded her to visit the healer a second time. She did, and that time she felt herself drawn into a trance. Furniture whirled about her, her mind reeled, and she began to speak, but not in her own voice. It was the voice of a dead girl named Chlorine.

Soon Leonora learned to enter into a trance at will. Over the next four years she was possessed by a number of spirits, each, it seemed, trying to gain control over her. They included the spirits of some famous people: actress Sara Siddons, poet Henry Wadsworth Longfellow, and composer Johann Sebastian Bach.

Leonora became the subject of a serious study. William James of Harvard College and Richard Hodgson of the American Society for Psychical Research "adopted" her. From 1887 until 1911, many people interested in spiritualism studied Leonora. Detectives trailed her. People copied down her every word. Every facet of her life was scrutinized for fraud. None was found.

During that time one spirit began to dominate Leonora in her trances. It was a spirit who called itself Dr. Phinuit. He spoke English with a heavy French accent.

In one of their tests, James and Hodgson assembled a group of people who were introduced to Leonora under false names. When Leonora dropped into a trance, Dr. Phinuit took over. He revealed details about the people that Leonora could not possibly have known—including places, dates, and even their real names. Every attempt to throw her off the track failed. The same test was conducted in England by members of the British Society for Psychical Research, with the same results.

As one final test, Oliver Lodge, head of the British committee, devised a test he felt would be foolproof. Lodge, it seems, had twin uncles, Robert and Jerry. Jerry had died twenty years earlier. At a séance Lodge showed Dr. Phinuit a gold watch. The doctor spoke at once. "It belonged to your uncle," he said. "Your Uncle Jerry." Then followed a rambling conversation between Lodge and Dr. Phinuit, during which the doctor revealed an astonishing number of anecdotes about the dead Uncle Jerry. Lodge was convinced that Leonora was an extraordinary medium.

At the conclusion of the séances, Oliver Lodge and his fellow committee members wrote a detailed report to the British society. They concluded that they had never met anyone like Leonora Piper. They were in awe of her powers.

As for Dr. Phinuit, however, the report stated that he was never a real person. The story of his life was contradictory. His medical knowledge was weak. Phinuit, the report suggested, was a variant of the name used by the Boston psychic whom Leonora first saw. Dr. Phinuit, they concluded, was Leonora's *alter ego*—another side of her personality that she got in touch with only when she entered a trance. She gave him his name unconsciously. There was no attempt at fraud. Her contact with spirits, the British group believed, was genuine. ■

*If you have been timed while reading this selection, enter your reading time below. Then turn to the Words per Minute table on page 155 and look up your reading speed (words per minute). Enter your reading speed on the graph on page 156.*

READING TIME: Unit 21

_____ : _____
*Minutes*        *Seconds*

# How well did you read?

- *Answer the four types of questions that follow. The directions for each type of question tell you how to mark your answers.*

- *When you have finished all four exercises, check your work by using the answer key on page 152. For each right answer, put a check mark (✔) on the line beside the box. For each wrong answer, write the correct answer on the line.*

- *For scoring each exercise, follow the directions below the questions.*

## A  FINDING THE MAIN IDEA

Look at the three statements below. One expresses the main idea of the story you just read. A good main idea statement answers two questions: it tells *who* or *what* is the subject of the story, and it answers the understood question *does what?* or *is what?* Another statement is *too broad,* it is vague and doesn't tell much about the topic of the story. The third statement is *too narrow,* it tells about only one part of the story.

Match the statements with the three answer choices below by writing the letter of each answer in the box in front of the statement it goes with.

**M—Main Idea**     **B—Too Broad**     **N—Too Narrow**

_____ ☐ 1. The Fox sisters were responsible for the birth of spiritualism.

_____ ☐ 2. The spiritualism movement included both frauds and apparently true mediums.

_____ ☐ 3. The spiritualism movement raised many questions about the ability of spirits to contact the living.

_____ Score 15 points for a correct *M* answer

_____ Score 5 points for each correct *B* or *N* answer

_____ TOTAL SCORE: Finding the Main Idea

## B  RECALLING FACTS

How well do you remember the facts in the story you just read? Put an *x* in the box in front of the correct answer to each of the multiple choice questions below.

1. The Fox sisters lived in
   - ☐ a. England.
   - ☐ b. New York.
   - ☐ c. the Midwest.

2. According to Margaret Fox, the rappings were made by
   - ☐ a. Dr. Phinuit.
   - ☐ b. snapping her fingers.
   - ☐ c. cracking her toe.

3. When Margaret Fox admitted to fraud,
   - ☐ a. the belief in spiritualism continued anyway.
   - ☐ b. she and her sisters were put in jail.
   - ☐ c. the spiritualism movement ended.

4. The spiritualism movement was strong during the
   - ☐ a. first half of the nineteenth century.
   - ☐ b. last half of the nineteenth century.
   - ☐ c. early twentieth century.

5. When in a trance, Leonora Piper could
   - ☐ a. speak foreign languages.
   - ☐ b. read minds.
   - ☐ c. identify strangers.

Score 5 points for each correct answer

_____ TOTAL SCORE: Recalling Facts

## C  MAKING INFERENCES

An inference is a judgment that is made or an idea that is arrived at based on facts or on information that is given. You make an inference when you understand something that is *not* stated directly, but that is *implied*, or suggested by the facts that are given.

Below are five statements that are judgments or ideas that have been arrived at from the facts of the story. Write the letter *C* in the box in front of each statement that is a correct inference. Write the letter *F* in front of each faulty inference.

**C—Correct Inference      F—Faulty Inference**

_____ ☐ 1. Leonora Piper is the only medium ever found to be honest.

_____ ☐ 2. The Fox sisters all felt guilty for the fraud they engaged in.

_____ ☐ 3. In the beginning, Margaret secretly told her two sisters about the trick of cracking her toe.

_____ ☐ 4. The psychic researchers forced Leonora to subject herself to their tests.

_____ ☐ 5. Many people are fascinated with the subject of spirits.

Score 5 points for each correct answer

_____ TOTAL SCORE: Making Inferences

## D USING WORDS PRECISELY

Each of the numbered sentences below contains an underlined word or phrase from the story you have just read. Under the sentence are three definitions. One has the *same* meaning as the underlined word or phrase, one has *almost the same* meaning, and one has the *opposite* meaning. Match the definitions with the three answer choices by writing the letter that stands for each answer in the box in front of the definition it goes with.

**S—Same     A—Almost the Same     O—Opposite**

1. Then, on March 31, after the family had gone to bed, the rappings started up and were so persistent that no one could sleep.

____ ☐ a. nagging

____ ☐ b. continuing

____ ☐ c. short-lived

2. Indeed, the harder the skeptics tried to discredit the Fox sisters, the more firmly their supporters believed.

____ ☐ a. cast doubt on

____ ☐ b. prove true

____ ☐ c. insult

3. You might think that this astonishing revelation spelled the end of spiritualism, but it didn't.

____ ☐ a. information

____ ☐ b. uncovering

____ ☐ c. secret

4. Only the wily Leah was able to go on, and she did, amassing a small fortune.

____ ☐ a. innocent

____ ☐ b. shrewd

____ ☐ c. sneaky

5. During that time one spirit began to dominate Leonora in her trances.

____ ☐ a. influence

____ ☐ b. serve

____ ☐ c. control

____ Score 3 points for each correct *S* answer
____ Score 1 point for each correct *A* or *O* answer

____ **TOTAL SCORE: Using Words Precisely**

- *Enter the four total scores in the spaces below, and add them together to find your Critical Reading Score. Then record your Critical Reading Score on the graph on page 157.*

_____ Finding the Main Idea
_____ Recalling Facts
_____ Making Inferences
_____ Using Words Precisely
_____ **CRITICAL READING SCORE: Unit 21**

# ANSWER KEY

## 1 The Bell Witch
A. Finding the Main Idea
1. N   2. M   3. B
B. Recalling Facts
1. c   2. c   3. a   4. b   5. c
C. Making Inferences
1. F   2. F   3. F   4. C   5. C
D. Using Words Precisely
1. a. A  b. S  c. O
2. a. S  b. A  c. O
3. a. O  b. S  c. A
4. a. O  b. A  c. S
5. a. A  b. O  c. S

## 2 The Gray Man of Pawley's Island
A. Finding the Main Idea
1. M   2. N   3. B
B. Recalling Facts
1. b   2. c   3. b   4. a   5. c
C. Making Inferences
1. C   2. C   3. F   4. F   5. C
D. Using Words Precisely
1. a. S  b. O  c. A
2. a. A  b. O  c. S
3. a. S  b. A  c. O
4. a. A  b. S  c. O
5. a. A  b. O  c. S

## 3 The Flying Dutchman
A. Finding the Main Idea
1. N   2. B   3. M
B. Recalling Facts
1. b   2. c   3. c   4. a   5. b
C. Making Inferences
1. C   2. C   3. C   4. F   5. F
D. Using Words Precisely
1. a. A  b. S  c. O
2. a. S  b. O  c. A
3. a. O  b. A  c. S
4. a. A  b. S  c. O
5. a. S  b. A  c. O

## 4 The Ghosts of Flight 401
A. Finding the Main Idea
1. B   2. M   3. N
B. Recalling Facts
1. a   2. a   3. a   4. c   5. b
C. Making Inferences
1. F   2. C   3. F   4. F   5. C
D. Using Words Precisely
1. a. O  b. S  c. A
2. a. A  b. O  c. S
3. a. O  b. S  c. A
4. a. A  b. O  c. S
5. a. S  b. A  c. O

## 5 Ocean-born Mary
A. Finding the Main Idea
1. B   2. N   3. M
B. Recalling Facts
1. b   2. b   3. a   4. a   5. c
C. Making Inferences
1. F   2. F   3. C   4. C   5. F
D. Using Words Precisely
1. a. S  b. A  c. O
2. a. A  b. O  c. S
3. a. O  b. A  c. S
4. a. S  b. O  c. A
5. a. A  b. S  c. O

## 6 The Case of the Missing Secretary
A. Finding the Main Idea
1. M   2. N   3. B
B. Recalling Facts
1. b   2. b   3. c   4. b   5. a
C. Making Inferences
1. C   2. F   3. C   4. F   5. C
D. Using Words Precisely
1. a. O  b. S  c. A
2. a. S  b. O  c. A
3. a. O  b. A  c. S
4. a. A  b. S  c. O
5. a. A  b. S  c. O

## 7 The Ghost Ship of Matthew Lee
A. Finding the Main Idea
1. N   2. B   3. M
B. Recalling Facts
1. b   2. a   3. c   4. b   5. a
C. Making Inferences
1. F   2. F   3. C   4. F   5. C
D. Using Words Precisely
1. a. S  b. A  c. O
2. a. A  b. O  c. S
3. a. S  b. O  c. A
4. a. O  b. S  c. A
5. a. O  b. A  c. S

## 8 Osceola's Head

A. Finding the Main Idea
   1. **N**    2. **M**    3. **B**

B. Recalling Facts
   1. a    2. a    3. c    4. b    5. a

C. Making Inferences
   1. **F**    2. **C**    3. **C**    4. **C**    5. **F**

D. Using Words Precisely
   1. a. **A**    b. **S**    c. **O**
   2. a. **A**    b. **O**    c. **S**
   3. a. **A**    b. **S**    c. **O**
   4. a. **O**    b. **A**    c. **S**
   5. a. **O**    b. **S**    c. **A**

## 9 Whaley House

A. Finding the Main Idea
   1. **B**    2. **N**    3. **M**

B. Recalling Facts
   1. c    2. a    3. c    4. a    5. b

C. Making Inferences
   1. **C**    2. **C**    3. **C**    4. **F**    5. **F**

D. Using Words Precisely
   1. a. **S**    b. **O**    c. **A**
   2. a. **S**    b. **O**    c. **A**
   3. a. **S**    b. **A**    c. **O**
   4. a. **O**    b. **S**    c. **A**
   5. a. **O**    b. **S**    c. **A**

## 10 The Marine Lieutenant's Ghost

A. Finding the Main Idea
   1. **B**    2. **M**    3. **N**

B. Recalling Facts
   1. a    2. b    3. a    4. c    5. a

C. Making Inferences
   1. **C**    2. **F**    3. **F**    4. **F**    5. **C**

D. Using Words Precisely
   1. a. **S**    b. **O**    c. **A**
   2. a. **A**    b. **O**    c. **S**
   3. a. **A**    b. **S**    c. **O**
   4. a. **S**    b. **O**    c. **A**
   5. a. **S**    b. **O**    c. **A**

## 11 The Haunted Gold Mine

A. Finding the Main Idea
   1. **B**    2. **N**    3. **M**

B. Recalling Facts
   1. b    2. b    3. c    4. a    5. b

C. Making Inferences
   1. **F**    2. **F**    3. **F**    4. **C**    5. **C**

D. Using Words Precisely
   1. a. **O**    b. **S**    c. **A**
   2. a. **O**    b. **S**    c. **A**
   3. a. **A**    b. **S**    c. **O**
   4. a. **A**    b. **S**    c. **O**
   5. a. **O**    b. **A**    c. **S**

## 12 Sarah's Ghost House

A. Finding the Main Idea
   1. **N**    2. **B**    3. **M**

B. Recalling Facts
   1. c    2. b    3. a    4. b    5. c

C. Making Inferences
   1. **F**    2. **F**    3. **C**    4. **F**    5. **C**

D. Using Words Precisely
   1. a. **A**    b. **S**    c. **O**
   2. a. **S**    b. **O**    c. **A**
   3. a. **A**    b. **O**    c. **S**
   4. a. **S**    b. **A**    c. **O**
   5. a. **A**    b. **S**    c. **O**

## 13 The Ghost Ship of Georges Bank

A. Finding the Main Idea
   1. **M**    2. **N**    3. **B**

B. Recalling Facts
   1. a    2. c    3. a    4. c    5. c

C. Making Inferences
   1. **C**    2. **C**    3. **C**    4. **F**    5. **F**

D. Using Words Precisely
   1. a. **S**    b. **A**    c. **O**
   2. a. **A**    b. **S**    c. **O**
   3. a. **O**    b. **S**    c. **A**
   4. a. **O**    b. **A**    c. **S**
   5. a. **S**    b. **O**    c. **A**

## 14 Harvey of Fort Sam Houston

A. Finding the Main Idea
   1. **B**    2. **N**    3. **M**

B. Recalling Facts
   1. b    2. c    3. a    4. c    5. b

C. Making Inferences
   1. **F**    2. **F**    3. **C**    4. **F**    5. **C**

D. Using Words Precisely
   1. a. **O**    b. **A**    c. **S**
   2. a. **A**    b. **S**    c. **O**
   3. a. **S**    b. **A**    c. **O**
   4. a. **A**    b. **S**    c. **O**
   5. a. **S**    b. **O**    c. **A**

### 15 The Return of Nelly Butler
A. Finding the Main Idea
1. **M**   2. **N**   3. **B**
B. Recalling Facts
1. **a**   2. **c**   3. **b**   4. **c**   5. **a**
C. Making Inferences
1. **F**   2. **F**   3. **C**   4. **C**   5. **F**
D. Using Words Precisely
1. a. **S**   b. **A**   c. **O**
2. a. **A**   b. **O**   c. **S**
3. a. **O**   b. **S**   c. **A**
4. a. **A**   b. **O**   c. **S**
5. a. **S**   b. **O**   c. **A**

### 16 A Beverly Hills Ghost
A. Finding the Main Idea
1. **M**   2. **B**   3. **N**
B. Recalling Facts
1. **b**   2. **a**   3. **c**   4. **b**   5. **a**
C. Making Inferences
1. **C**   2. **C**   3. **F**   4. **F**   5. **F**
D. Using Words Precisely
1. a. **O**   b. **S**   c. **A**
2. a. **S**   b. **O**   c. **A**
3. a. **A**   b. **O**   c. **S**
4. a. **S**   b. **A**   c. **O**
5. a. **A**   b. **O**   c. **S**

### 17 The Haunted U-Boat
A. Finding the Main Idea
1. **N**   2. **B**   3. **M**
B. Recalling Facts
1. **a**   2. **b**   3. **a**   4. **b**   5. **b**
C. Making Inferences
1. **C**   2. **F**   3. **F**   4. **C**   5. **F**
D. Using Words Precisely
1. a. **O**   b. **S**   c. **A**
2. a. **O**   b. **A**   c. **S**
3. a. **A**   b. **S**   c. **O**
4. a. **O**   b. **S**   c. **A**
5. a. **A**   b. **S**   c. **O**

### 18 Lady in Black
A. Finding the Main Idea
1. **N**   2. **B**   3. **M**
B. Recalling Facts
1. **b**   2. **b**   3. **b**   4. **a**   5. **b**
C. Making Inferences
1. **F**   2. **F**   3. **C**   4. **C**   5. **F**
D. Using Words Precisely
1. a. **S**   b. **O**   c. **A**
2. a. **A**   b. **S**   c. **O**
3. a. **A**   b. **S**   c. **O**
4. a. **A**   b. **O**   c. **S**
5. a. **S**   b. **A**   c. **O**

### 19 The Yankee Poltergeist
A. Finding the Main Idea
1. **M**   2. **N**   3. **B**
B. Recalling Facts
1. **b**   2. **a**   3. **c**   4. **c**   5. **b**
C. Making Inferences
1. **F**   2. **C**   3. **F**   4. **C**   5. **C**
D. Using Words Precisely
1. a. **A**   b. **O**   c. **S**
2. a. **O**   b. **S**   c. **A**
3. a. **A**   b. **S**   c. **O**
4. a. **A**   b. **O**   c. **S**
5. a. **S**   b. **A**   c. **O**

### 20 Testimony of a Ghost in Court
A. Finding the Main Idea
1. **M**   2. **B**   3. **N**
B. Recalling Facts
1. **b**   2. **a**   3. **c**   4. **b**   5. **a**
C. Making Inferences
1. **C**   2. **F**   3. **F**   4. **C**   5. **C**
D. Using Words Precisely
1. a. **S**   b. **O**   c. **A**
2. a. **O**   b. **A**   c. **S**
3. a. **S**   b. **A**   c. **O**
4. a. **S**   b. **O**   c. **A**
5. a. **O**   b. **S**   c. **A**

### 21 Spiritualism: Fact or Fraud?
A. Finding the Main Idea
1. **N**   2. **M**   3. **B**
B. Recalling Facts
1. **b**   2. **c**   3. **a**   4. **b**   5. **c**
C. Making Inferences
1. **F**   2. **F**   3. **C**   4. **F**   5. **C**
D. Using Words Precisely
1. a. **A**   b. **S**   c. **O**
2. a. **S**   b. **O**   c. **A**
3. a. **A**   b. **S**   c. **O**
4. a. **O**   b. **S**   c. **A**
5. a. **A**   b. **O**   c. **S**

# WORDS PER MINUTE TABLE
# & PROGRESS GRAPHS

# Words per Minute

|  | GROUP ONE | | | | | | | |  |
| --- | --- | --- | --- | --- | --- | --- | --- | --- | --- |
| Unit ▶ | Sample | 1 | 2 | 3 | 4 | 5 | 6 | 7 |  |
| No. of Words ▶ | 879 | 1652 | 931 | 1296 | 1256 | 1443 | 1479 | 1039 |  |
| 1:30 | 586 | 1101 | 621 | 864 | 837 | 962 | 986 | 693 | 90 |
| 1:40 | 527 | 991 | 559 | 778 | 754 | 866 | 887 | 623 | 100 |
| 1:50 | 479 | 901 | 508 | 707 | 685 | 787 | 807 | 567 | 110 |
| 2:00 | 440 | 826 | 466 | 648 | 628 | 722 | 740 | 520 | 120 |
| 2:10 | 406 | 762 | 430 | 598 | 580 | 666 | 683 | 480 | 130 |
| 2:20 | 377 | 708 | 399 | 555 | 538 | 618 | 634 | 445 | 140 |
| 2:30 | 352 | 661 | 372 | 518 | 502 | 577 | 592 | 416 | 150 |
| 2:40 | 330 | 620 | 349 | 486 | 471 | 541 | 555 | 390 | 160 |
| 2:50 | 310 | 583 | 329 | 457 | 443 | 509 | 522 | 367 | 170 |
| 3:00 | 293 | 551 | 310 | 432 | 419 | 481 | 493 | 346 | 180 |
| 3:10 | 278 | 522 | 294 | 409 | 397 | 456 | 467 | 328 | 190 |
| 3:20 | 264 | 496 | 279 | 389 | 377 | 433 | 444 | 312 | 200 |
| 3:30 | 251 | 472 | 266 | 370 | 359 | 412 | 423 | 297 | 210 |
| 3:40 | 240 | 451 | 254 | 353 | 343 | 394 | 403 | 283 | 220 |
| 3:50 | 230 | 431 | 243 | 338 | 328 | 376 | 386 | 271 | 230 |
| 4:00 | 220 | 413 | 233 | 324 | 314 | 361 | 370 | 260 | 240 |
| 4:10 | 211 | 396 | 223 | 311 | 301 | 346 | 355 | 249 | 250 |
| 4:20 | 203 | 381 | 215 | 299 | 290 | 333 | 341 | 240 | 260 |
| 4:30 | 195 | 367 | 207 | 288 | 279 | 321 | 329 | 231 | 270 |
| 4:40 | 188 | 354 | 200 | 278 | 269 | 309 | 317 | 223 | 280 |
| 4:50 | 182 | 342 | 193 | 268 | 260 | 299 | 306 | 215 | 290 |
| 5:00 | 176 | 330 | 186 | 259 | 251 | 289 | 296 | 208 | 300 |
| 5:10 | 170 | 320 | 180 | 251 | 243 | 279 | 286 | 201 | 310 |
| 5:20 | 165 | 310 | 175 | 243 | 236 | 271 | 277 | 195 | 320 |
| 5:30 | 160 | 300 | 169 | 236 | 228 | 262 | 269 | 189 | 330 |
| 5:40 | 155 | 292 | 165 | 229 | 222 | 255 | 261 | 183 | 340 |
| 5:50 | 151 | 283 | 160 | 222 | 215 | 247 | 254 | 178 | 350 |
| 6:00 | 147 | 275 | 155 | 216 | 209 | 241 | 247 | 173 | 360 |
| 6:10 | 143 | 268 | 151 | 210 | 204 | 234 | 240 | 168 | 370 |
| 6:20 | 139 | 261 | 147 | 205 | 198 | 228 | 234 | 164 | 380 |
| 6:30 | 135 | 254 | 143 | 199 | 193 | 222 | 228 | 160 | 390 |
| 6:40 | 132 | 248 | 140 | 194 | 188 | 216 | 222 | 156 | 400 |
| 6:50 | 129 | 242 | 136 | 190 | 184 | 211 | 216 | 152 | 410 |
| 7:00 | 126 | 236 | 133 | 185 | 179 | 206 | 211 | 148 | 420 |
| 7:20 | 120 | 225 | 127 | 177 | 171 | 197 | 202 | 142 | 440 |
| 7:40 | 115 | 215 | 121 | 169 | 164 | 188 | 193 | 136 | 460 |
| 8:00 | 110 | 207 | 116 | 162 | 157 | 180 | 185 | 130 | 480 |

Minutes and Seconds ▶

Seconds ◀

## GROUP TWO

| Unit ▶ | 8 | 9 | 10 | 11 | 12 | 13 | 14 | |
|---|---|---|---|---|---|---|---|---|
| No. of Words ▶ | 1128 | 1284 | 1486 | 1527 | 1471 | 1535 | 1268 | |
| 1:30 | 752 | 856 | 991 | 1018 | 981 | 1023 | 845 | 90 |
| 1:40 | 677 | 770 | 892 | 916 | 883 | 921 | 761 | 100 |
| 1:50 | 615 | 700 | 811 | 833 | 802 | 837 | 692 | 110 |
| 2:00 | 564 | 642 | 743 | 764 | 736 | 768 | 634 | 120 |
| 2:10 | 521 | 593 | 686 | 705 | 679 | 708 | 585 | 130 |
| 2:20 | 483 | 550 | 637 | 654 | 630 | 658 | 543 | 140 |
| 2:30 | 451 | 514 | 594 | 611 | 588 | 614 | 507 | 150 |
| 2:40 | 423 | 482 | 557 | 573 | 552 | 576 | 476 | 160 |
| 2:50 | 398 | 453 | 524 | 539 | 519 | 542 | 448 | 170 |
| 3:00 | 376 | 428 | 495 | 509 | 490 | 512 | 423 | 180 |
| 3:10 | 356 | 405 | 469 | 482 | 465 | 485 | 400 | 190 |
| 3:20 | 338 | 385 | 446 | 458 | 441 | 461 | 380 | 200 |
| 3:30 | 322 | 367 | 425 | 436 | 420 | 439 | 362 | 210 |
| 3:40 | 308 | 350 | 405 | 416 | 401 | 419 | 346 | 220 |
| 3:50 | 294 | 335 | 388 | 398 | 384 | 401 | 331 | 230 |
| 4:00 | 282 | 321 | 372 | 382 | 368 | 384 | 317 | 240 |
| 4:10 | 271 | 308 | 357 | 366 | 353 | 368 | 304 | 250 |
| 4:20 | 260 | 296 | 343 | 352 | 339 | 354 | 293 | 260 |
| 4:30 | 251 | 285 | 330 | 339 | 327 | 341 | 282 | 270 |
| 4:40 | 242 | 275 | 318 | 327 | 315 | 329 | 272 | 280 |
| 4:50 | 233 | 266 | 307 | 316 | 304 | 318 | 262 | 290 |
| 5:00 | 226 | 257 | 297 | 305 | 294 | 307 | 254 | 300 |
| 5:10 | 218 | 249 | 288 | 296 | 285 | 297 | 245 | 310 |
| 5:20 | 212 | 241 | 279 | 286 | 276 | 288 | 238 | 320 |
| 5:30 | 205 | 233 | 270 | 278 | 267 | 279 | 231 | 330 |
| 5:40 | 199 | 227 | 262 | 269 | 260 | 271 | 224 | 340 |
| 5:50 | 193 | 220 | 255 | 262 | 252 | 263 | 217 | 350 |
| 6:00 | 188 | 214 | 248 | 255 | 245 | 256 | 211 | 360 |
| 6:10 | 183 | 208 | 241 | 248 | 239 | 249 | 206 | 370 |
| 6:20 | 178 | 203 | 235 | 241 | 232 | 242 | 200 | 380 |
| 6:30 | 174 | 198 | 229 | 235 | 226 | 236 | 195 | 390 |
| 6:40 | 169 | 193 | 223 | 229 | 221 | 230 | 190 | 400 |
| 6:50 | 165 | 188 | 217 | 223 | 215 | 225 | 186 | 410 |
| 7:00 | 161 | 183 | 212 | 218 | 210 | 219 | 181 | 420 |
| 7:20 | 154 | 175 | 203 | 208 | 201 | 209 | 173 | 440 |
| 7:40 | 147 | 167 | 194 | 199 | 192 | 200 | 165 | 460 |
| 8:00 | 141 | 161 | 186 | 191 | 184 | 192 | 159 | 480 |

*Minutes and Seconds* / *Seconds*

## GROUP THREE

| Unit ▶ | 15 | 16 | 17 | 18 | 19 | 20 | 21 | |
|---|---|---|---|---|---|---|---|---|
| No. of Words ▶ | 1429 | 1386 | 1203 | 1521 | 1450 | 1198 | 1456 | |
| 1:30 | 953 | 924 | 802 | 1014 | 967 | 799 | 971 | 90 |
| 1:40 | 857 | 832 | 722 | 913 | 870 | 719 | 874 | 100 |
| 1:50 | 779 | 756 | 656 | 830 | 791 | 653 | 794 | 110 |
| 2:00 | 715 | 693 | 602 | 761 | 725 | 599 | 728 | 120 |
| 2:10 | 660 | 640 | 555 | 702 | 669 | 553 | 672 | 130 |
| 2:20 | 612 | 594 | 516 | 652 | 621 | 513 | 624 | 140 |
| 2:30 | 572 | 554 | 481 | 608 | 580 | 479 | 582 | 150 |
| 2:40 | 536 | 520 | 451 | 570 | 544 | 449 | 546 | 160 |
| 2:50 | 504 | 489 | 425 | 537 | 512 | 423 | 514 | 170 |
| 3:00 | 476 | 462 | 401 | 507 | 483 | 399 | 485 | 180 |
| 3:10 | 451 | 438 | 380 | 480 | 458 | 378 | 460 | 190 |
| 3:20 | 429 | 416 | 361 | 456 | 435 | 359 | 437 | 200 |
| 3:30 | 408 | 396 | 344 | 435 | 414 | 342 | 416 | 210 |
| 3:40 | 390 | 378 | 328 | 415 | 395 | 327 | 397 | 220 |
| 3:50 | 373 | 362 | 314 | 397 | 378 | 313 | 380 | 230 |
| 4:00 | 357 | 347 | 301 | 380 | 363 | 300 | 364 | 240 |
| 4:10 | 343 | 333 | 289 | 365 | 348 | 288 | 349 | 250 |
| 4:20 | 330 | 320 | 278 | 351 | 335 | 276 | 336 | 260 |
| 4:30 | 318 | 308 | 267 | 338 | 322 | 266 | 324 | 270 |
| 4:40 | 306 | 297 | 258 | 326 | 311 | 257 | 312 | 280 |
| 4:50 | 296 | 287 | 249 | 315 | 300 | 248 | 301 | 290 |
| 5:00 | 286 | 277 | 241 | 304 | 290 | 240 | 291 | 300 |
| 5:10 | 277 | 268 | 233 | 294 | 281 | 232 | 282 | 310 |
| 5:20 | 268 | 260 | 226 | 285 | 272 | 225 | 273 | 320 |
| 5:30 | 260 | 252 | 219 | 277 | 264 | 218 | 265 | 330 |
| 5:40 | 252 | 245 | 212 | 268 | 256 | 211 | 257 | 340 |
| 5:50 | 245 | 238 | 206 | 261 | 249 | 205 | 250 | 350 |
| 6:00 | 238 | 231 | 201 | 254 | 242 | 200 | 243 | 360 |
| 6:10 | 232 | 225 | 195 | 247 | 235 | 194 | 236 | 370 |
| 6:20 | 226 | 219 | 190 | 240 | 229 | 189 | 230 | 380 |
| 6:30 | 220 | 213 | 185 | 234 | 223 | 184 | 224 | 390 |
| 6:40 | 214 | 208 | 180 | 228 | 218 | 180 | 218 | 400 |
| 6:50 | 209 | 203 | 176 | 226 | 212 | 175 | 213 | 410 |
| 7:00 | 204 | 198 | 172 | 217 | 207 | 171 | 208 | 420 |
| 7:20 | 195 | 189 | 164 | 207 | 198 | 163 | 199 | 440 |
| 7:40 | 186 | 181 | 157 | 198 | 189 | 156 | 190 | 460 |
| 8:00 | 179 | 173 | 150 | 190 | 181 | 150 | 182 | 480 |

*Minutes and Seconds* / *Seconds*

# Reading Speed

**Directions:** *Write your Words per Minute score for each unit in the box under the number of the unit. Then plot your reading speed on the graph by putting a small* **x** *on the line directly above the number of the unit, across from the number of words per minute you read. As you mark your speed for each unit, graph your progress by drawing a line to connect the* **x**'s.

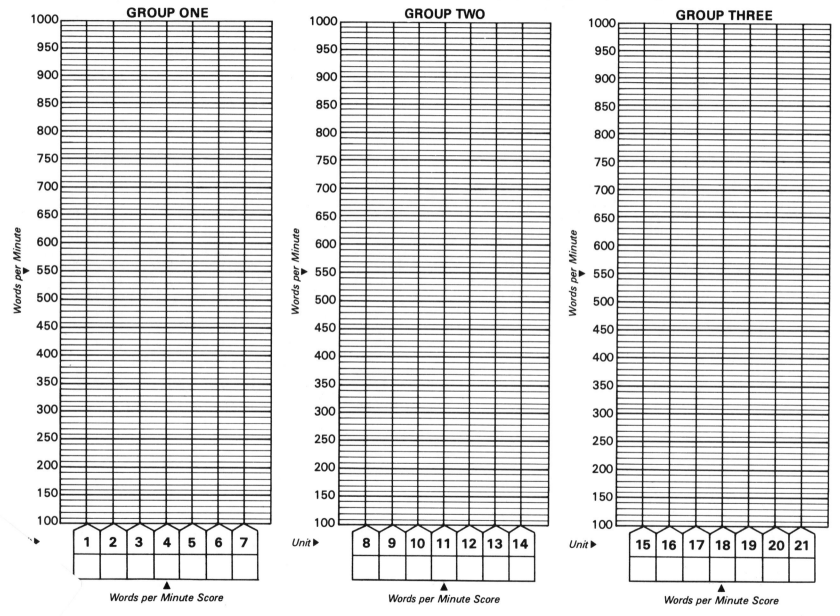

GROUP ONE

1000
950
900
850
800
750
700
650
Words per Minute ▶ 600
550
500
450
400
350
300
250
200
150
100

| 1 | 2 | 3 | 4 | 5 | 6 | 7 |
|---|---|---|---|---|---|---|
|   |   |   |   |   |   |   |

▲
Words per Minute Score

GROUP TWO

1000
950
900
850
800
750
700
650
Words per Minute ▶ 600
550
500
450
400
350
300
250
200
150
100

Unit ▶

| 8 | 9 | 10 | 11 | 12 | 13 | 14 |
|---|---|----|----|----|----|----|
|   |   |    |    |    |    |    |

▲
Words per Minute Score

GROUP THREE

1000
950
900
850
800
750
700
650
Words per Minute ▶ 600
550
500
450
400
350
300
250
200
150
100

Unit ▶

| 15 | 16 | 17 | 18 | 19 | 20 | 21 |
|----|----|----|----|----|----|----|
|    |    |    |    |    |    |    |

▲
Words per Minute Score

# Critical Reading Scores

**Directions:** *Write your Critical Reading Score for each unit in the box under the number of the unit. Then plot your score on the graph by putting a small **x** on the line directly above the number of the unit, across from the score you earned. As you mark your score for each unit, graph your progress by drawing a line to connect the **x**'s.*

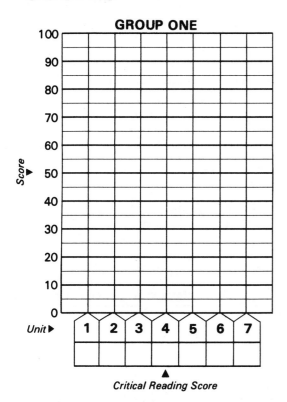

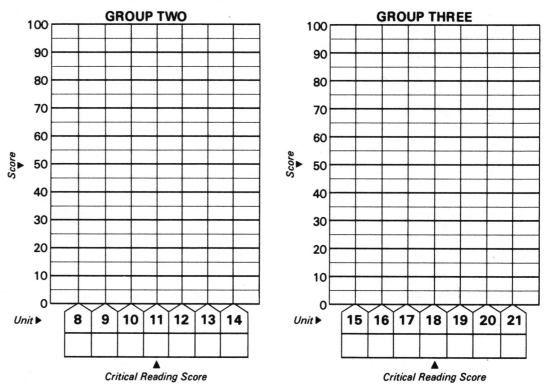

# Picture Credits